BEOWULF
and Other Old English Poems

BEOWULF
and Other Old English Poems

Translated by CONSTANCE B. HIEATT

With an introduction by A. Kent Hieatt

The Odyssey Press, Inc.
Bobbs-Merrill Educational Publishing
Indianapolis

The Bobbs-Merrill Company, Inc.
4300 West 62nd Street
Indianapolis, Indiana 46268

First Edition
Eighth Printing—1981
Library of Congress Catalog Card Number: 67-25645
ISBN 0-672-63012-5 (pbk)

⊸⊰ TRANSLATOR'S PREFACE ⊱⊸

This version of *Beowulf* is obviously not intended for an audience of scholars of Old English, for no translation can be a substitute for the original. Nor is it a trot for graduate students struggling to reach that eminence; the more-or-less literal translations of J. R. Clark-Hall, E. T. Donaldson, and E. V. Gordon are sufficient for their purposes. My aim has been simply to produce a readable translation for adult readers and college students who do not read Old English. A few shorter poems have also been included as some indication both of the quality and variety of Old English poetry and of its coherence as a body of literature; while all the shorter poems are quite different from *Beowulf* (and, in most cases, from each other), each has particular similarities, and all together can give a reader an idea of the literary context in which that great poem belongs.

Since readability was a primary objective, literal translation was out of the question. Therefore, while I have endeavored to be as faithful to the text as possible, I have taken a great many liberties in rearranging sentences, and have simply discarded some minor details (such as Wiglaf's kinship to Aelfhere) which may be interesting to the specialist but which add little or nothing for the modern reader unacquainted with the material.

Certain of the poetic embellishments (although not as many as in some translations) have also been sacrificed, since this is a prose translation. Working in prose cannot really be described as a decision, since I never seriously considered verse: it is my conviction that a verse translation may be a good poem, but it is not the *same* poem. The qualities which remain the same in a translation are those of theme and structure, and greater verbal accuracy is possible in a prose translation, where a faithful rendering of the meaning is not obscured by the exigencies of a superimposed verse form. The shorter poems are, of course, generally more lyric, and thus lend themselves less easily to prose translation. But even here it still seemed preferable to render their content as clearly as possible, without the obscuring effect of an alien verse convention.

There is one exception: *The Seafarer* is given in Ezra Pound's brilliant verse translation, or adaptation. If the reader will compare this poem with the prose translation of *The Wanderer,* a quite similar work, he may judge for himself the different advantages of prose and verse in translation.

Like the translations themselves, the notes were composed with a nonspecialist audience in mind. In general, I have given a note only when it seemed to me that the reader might be confused without it. I hope that the introduction will clear up many questions before they arise: a reader coming to *Beowulf* for the first time should certainly be urged to read the introduction first.

I am fortunate in being able to include an introduction by my husband, A. Kent Hieatt. It is difficult to express gratitude properly to one who is in effect a collaborator; I must simply say that we have both read each other's work and offered various suggestions for its improvement—most of which were accepted.

Gratitude is also due, of course, to many other scholars and teachers, but most of all to John C. Pope. I would dedicate the book to him if it did not seem an inadequate offering.

C. B. H.

❧ CONTENTS ❧

---❧ INTRODUCTION ❧--

All of the poems which are translated in this collection reached
the form in which we now have them between the seventh and
tenth centuries. They were composed in Old English, or Anglo-
Saxon, which was the earliest form of our language, preceding
Middle English, which was, for instance, the speech of Geoffrey
Chaucer (ca. 1340–1400). The small group of remarkable Old
English poems and prose works which survives is the earliest body
of literature in any of the vernaculars which have developed into
the modern languages of Europe.

Beowulf (summary of story on p. 8), the longest and most im-
portant poem here, concerns famous deeds supposedly performed
in an age long before that of the poet among Germanic tribes liv-
ing near the European homeland from which the Anglo-Saxons,
another Germanic folk, had come to England. Almost surely, it
was composed by a single author in the eighth century, after En-
gland had become Christianized but while pagan habits of
thought were still strong. It comes from the north of England—
either from the far north, then called Northumbria, where we
know there was a strong intellectual culture at the time, or from
what was known as Mercia, directly to the south of this.

We should not know of *Beowulf* at all if a single manuscript of
it had not survived the expropriation of the monasteries, with
their libraries, by Henry VIII in the sixteenth century, and a dis-
astrous library fire in 1731. This manuscript apparently dates
from the tenth century. Charred at the edges by the fire, it con-
tinues to deteriorate year by year. An edition of it prepared by

1

the Dane Thorkelin from copies made in 1787 preserved many words which have since disappeared from the original, but this edition was burned in the British bombardment of Copenhagen in 1807. Thorkelin's original copies, however, fortunately survived.

The history of *Beowulf's* physical preservation is, then, something of a cliff-hanger. The poem itself has been systematically studied only during a recent part of its long existence. As a consequence of this study the estimate of this work's significance has undergone mutations almost as sensational as the manuscript's survival of the burning of Robert Cotton's library. It is now almost customary to begin writing about it by condemning earlier commentators. This is possibly as it should be, for *Beowulf* even today is the most drastically misunderstood of all the monuments of English literature. Furthermore, it is so difficult to say what the work really amounts to that it is easiest to begin by smothering in the cradle some easily conceived false ideas that arise from mating it with quite different kinds of poems, or from judging it by literary standards irrelevant to its highly individual kind of life.

One of the best and most influential essays ever written about *Beowulf* states absolutely that it is a lyric, not a narrative, poem. This is possibly intentional exaggeration, but what the writer, Professor J. R. R. Tolkien (see Bibliography), probably meant was that the poem is a tissue of oblique allusions and highly stylized elegiac passages intended to build a particular atmosphere and a particular feeling about life, more than it is a straight narration of a series of events in the life of a hero. This claim is surely true; *Beowulf* cannot be considered an epic like the *Iliad*. It is just as true, moreover, that in spite of its calamitous ending this poem is not a "tragedy" in the sense in which the *Iliad* or Sophocles' *Oedipus the King* or *Hamlet* is a tragedy, or in the sense in which Aristotle said tragedies ought to function. Its hero has no specific tragic flaw precipitating his downfall; his only flaw is the most general one that he belongs to humankind and is subject to our common fate. On the other hand *Beowulf* is not simply a myth or a piece of folklore, for it is a product of sophisticated literary calculation. And it is not an allegory of good and evil, as so much medieval literature is, for the warfare which forms its background is not an *abstract* illustration of ethical problems; some of this strife is certainly historical, and much more may be.

One reason that *Beowulf* is difficult to describe as a piece of literature is that it had no successors and that nothing like it survives. It is true, of course, that the very local Germanic language in which it was written has gone on from strength to strength until in its modern forms it is the most important language in the world; but the great body of partly heathen, partly Christian Germanic poetry and prose to which *Beowulf* belongs became a closed system long ago.

The Germanic peoples of the Dark Ages had a shared tradition of oral compositions stretching from Austria and Northern France north and west to Scandinavia and Iceland. If we consider this body of works in terms of what was written down and survived, we may say that it begins with Old English literature (seventh–eleventh centuries), continues in the material of the Icelandic Edda and sagas (eleventh–thirteenth centuries) and in some less important German and Scandinavian material, and closes with the Austro-German *Nibelungenlied* (ca. 1204). Efforts to revive this literature or imitate it have been interesting in themselves but have missed its true quality. The Germanic dragon slayer Sigemund of *Beowulf,* for instance, some of whose attributes are those of the Sigurd of the Icelandic *Volsungasaga,* and of the Sifrit of the *Nibelungenlied,* is apparently revived in the Siegfried of Wagnerian opera, but Wagner's Siegfried and Brunhilde affect us in the way of some early Germanic literature only at a kind of mythical, preliterary level. The development of the narrative and stylistic traditions of later English, and all other, poetry and fiction really lies outside the influence of this Germanic literature. Even the Old English alliterative verse forms scarcely survived after the century of Chaucer, the fourteenth, when they came back briefly into surviving writings in the highly altered form of *Sir Gawain and the Green Knight* and some other poems in the north and west of England. That was nearly the end, except, perhaps, for the point that English poetry alliterates more to this day than poetry does in most other languages.

Even within the total body of early Germanic literature, *Beo-*

wulf stands by itself in many important respects. Icelandic saga, for instance, is severely objective in its narrative: authorial comment and point of view are so muted that even the modern reader is likely to lose his bearings. *Beowulf,* on the other hand, is commentary through and through, in several senses. Sometimes the commentary is very sly, in the sense that one section of the story inconspicuously contrasts with or parallels another, or that an interpolated story or allusion has some kind of many-layered reference to the main action. At other times the commentary is very straightforward, as when the character King Hrothgar makes ethical pronouncements worthy of another Dane, Polonius, or when the author himself is performing one of his bracing exercises in differentiating the sheep from the goats. (He consigns nicors, dragons, ungenerous kinglets, cruel queens, Cain-descended beings, and cowardly retainers to darkness, mist, slime, fens, caves, and perdition with a heart-warming gusto and rhetorical amplitude; the rest of us, on the other hand, are made to seem sons of light. The author's aims are really far from being simple-minded, but he is against evil with the muscular conviction of a muckraking newspaper.)

Here, certainly, the objectivity of Icelandic saga furnishes no parallel, either to *Beowulf* or to most of the rest of Old English poetry, which almost always shares in this militant glorification of good over evil; some Old English poems display, in fact, a kind of rhetorical wallowing in this contrast. But even if we narrow the focus from Germanic literature in general to Old English literature in particular, the rest of this highly interesting Old English poetry is of only a little help in understanding what is most important about *Beowulf* in a literary sense.

What other Old English poetry most obviously shares with *Beowulf* is a system of versification. In this system, end rhyme almost never appears. Unless a line is defective, it has four beats or, technically, "lifts"; there is a pause in the middle of the line; and the sound at the beginning of the syllable carrying the third lift also appears at (i.e., alliterates with) the beginning of the first lift, or of the second lift, or of both of them, but never at the beginning of the fourth lift (alliterating lifts are italicized here):

Swa begnornodon   *Geata* leode
1   2   3   4

*hla*fordes *hryre*,   *heorth*-geneatas;
1   2   3   4

cwædon thæt he *wære*   *wyr*uld-cyninga,
1   2   3   4

*man*na *mild*ust   ond *mon*-thwærust,
1   2   3 4

*leod*um *'lith*ost   ond *lof*-geornost.
1   2   3 4

In the feet (iambs, trochees, anapests, dactyls) of most poems likely to be familiar to the reader, the number of unaccented syllables is theoretically constant, but in Old English poetry the number of unaccented syllables between the lifts typically varies. In the final five lines of *Beowulf*, which are quoted above, there is no syllable at all between the last two lifts in the last two lines. This kind of verse was traditionally recited aloud, not read silently. It seems likely that the note of a harp was used to substitute for spoken syllables at some points in the pattern. For instance, in the first line above, such a note (indicated below by a rest substituting for a musical quarter note) probably supplied the first lift. According to the most popular theory today,[1] each quarter of a line with its lift was heard as a measure in 2/4 musical time, here indicated by quarter and eighth notes:

Aside from versification, certain shared stylistic traits (discussed below) make *Beowulf* and all other Old English poems sound superficially rather alike. Nevertheless, *Beowulf* remains sig-

---

[1] That of John C. Pope, most simply explained in *Seven Old English Poems*, edited by him (Bobbs-Merrill Library of Literature, 1966).

nificantly different. The only other complete poem in Old English which deals with the deeds of Germanic heroes is *Deor,* but this is a short lyric. It is a remarkable lament, but it is not, as *Beowulf* is, a long narrative *about* these deeds. *The Wanderer* and *The Seafarer* are similarly short, wonderfully evocative lyrics, among the best and most famous in Old English, but they are not at all concerned with traditional Germanic heroes. The deeds of such heroes are related in other Germanic languages of the Middle Ages, but, as was indicated, the poems or prose works in which these relations appear are so different from *Beowulf* that they do not much help our understanding of the poem as a work of art. On the other hand, the Old English *Maldon* and *Brunanburh* are outstanding narrative poems, like *Beowulf,* but they are much shorter, and each of them is about one battle within the immediate historical range of the poet, not about some semi-mythical past. *Waldere* and *Finnsburh* do enter that past, but are merely tantalizing fragments of lost longer poems. Other Old English poems are built on far different material borrowed from outside the Germanic world. The Old Testament is drawn on and adapted in Genesis and Exodus, and in *Judith,* a very powerful fragment. Saints' lives from the Mediterranean world appear in *Andreas* and *Elene,* and the allegorized story of a non-Germanic miraculous bird in *The Phoenix.* From the New Testament the story and significance of Christ's crucifixion is fervently rendered in *The Dream of the Rood,* perhaps the most remarkable of Old English devotional poems.

Great as these poems are, none of them really comes near what many students of the subject now recognize as the essential artistry of *Beowulf,* although there is one interesting qualification here: all these poems, whatever the subject, make use of some of the heroic habits of thought which *Beowulf* shares. For instance, the Cross, imagined as speaking in *The Dream of the Rood,* describes a Christ who is active and warriorlike in his crucifixion, which sounds like a battle:

> The young Hero—who was God almighty—stripped Himself. Strong and resolute, He ascended onto the high gallows while many beheld His courage, when He wished to free mankind. I trembled when the Warrior embraced me . . . . They drove dark nails through me: the open wounds, inflicted in malice, are still visible.

Christ's followers conduct his death rites as though they were Germanic warriors:

> Then they took almighty God and lifted Him up from the heavy punishment . . . . They laid down the weary-limbed Warrior and stood by the head of His body, beholding there Heaven's Lord. There He rested a while, spent after the great ordeal. Still within view of His bane, they began to build Him a sepulchre. They carved it of bright stone, and set the Ruler of victories in it; the mourners began to sing a dirge as evening approached, until time came for them to go off, weary, leaving the glorious Lord to rest there with scant company.
>
> But still we stood there in that same place, mourning, for a long time. The voices of the warriors faded away. The body, fair dwelling of the soul, grew cold.

It is only in two strictly speaking nonliterary respects that most Germanic narratives—Old English, Icelandic saga, the *Nibelung-enlied*—share something important with *Beowulf*. A reader needs to know about these points in order to understand the poem. The first of these is the frequent similarity of narrative motifs—much the same heroes, much the same incidents—often appearing in widely separated times and places. The Germanic peoples seem to have inherited a common body of narrative, which is a key to understanding the often incomplete and puzzling allusions and interpolated stories forming a large part of *Beowulf*. The other feature which *Beowulf* shares with other Germanic narratives is an emphasis upon the ethical principle of loyalty to another—to friend, family, chieftain, tribe, or the company of all faithful Christians (one of the clearest illustrations of this principle is *Maldon*). The breaking of this bond through cowardice or treachery is considered singularly abominable; and personally executed revenge—no matter how long delayed, no matter how sanguinary—against the ones who harm one's associates is held to be mandatory for every man, unless he is to be shamed publicly and even to hate himself. The typical tragedy of the Icelandic sagas is that of the good and far-seeing man who will not stir for small causes, even when his wife taunts him and his sons press weapons into his hands, but who, knowing he will sooner or later be murdered in turn, will kill coldly and kill again when this vengeful necessity of his manhood and fame is finally thrust upon him by the folly of others. In the same way, the pathos of the *Nibelungenlied* lies in the working out of a devious pattern of mutual vengeance through hecatombs of frightful slaughter. The author himself sees that loyalty so understood is self-defeating, but he shows us no alternative. The Old English poems adapting Old Testament materials often center around much the same idea of vengeance: for example, the heroine of *Judith* cuts Holofernes' throat as a revenge for the Israelites, Satan revenges himself on God by attempting to destroy mankind, and God revenges himself on the Egyptians for the sake of his chosen people.

Liberal opinion is, of course, in full flight from this general principle, although each of us must recognize its force, inwardly in himself and outwardly in the feud, in the vendetta, and in much of the history of our own country and the world. We know that this principle is taken for granted in any society organized tribally and in terms of bloodlines and lacking legal remedy. Loyalty and bloody deeds of vengeance are preoccupations in much of the world's literature, not least in the later, feudal Middle Ages, in which the division of Lancelot's or Tristram's loyalty between the queen whom he loves and the king whom he serves is a famous case in point. But Germanic story probably makes more of this doubtful ideal than does any other narrative tradition.

Beowulf, admittedly, shares in this doctrine of particular loyalties and of personal and social vengeance, and in the literary habit of extracting pathos from these patterns, but with a vital difference. In *Beowulf* alone these ideals appear in a partly sublimated and palatable form—institutionalized, so to speak, and harnessed into the service of a permanently acceptable view of man's lot, not of our primitive urges solely.

Beowulf's own loyalty, it is true, is literally tribal and familial. In the foreground of the story, the young hero, a nephew of the king of the Geats in Sweden, goes to the Danes, with whose kings he has connections, destroys the Dane-devouring monster Grendel, destroys Grendel's mother (who has executed an unlooked-for vengeance herself), returns to the Geats, serves his king and the latter's successors, becomes king himself, and in his old age kills and is killed by a dragon who had been destroying the Geats. In the background of the story, the hero is even caught up in self-destructive tribal war, just as certain loyal warriors of the *Nibelun-*

genlied or a wife-ridden Icelandic hero is drawn into the execution of vengeance. Beowulf fights the Frisians because his rash king leads him among them; he fights the Swedes because his tribe has inherited a pattern of vengeance and countervengeance against them.

In reality, however, this pattern of personal and tribal loyalties is generalized. The *Beowulf* author's intention is to define the preeminent man as such, who is generous and helpful to those around him and gains his fame by such acts. In the foreground he fights the enemies of us all, not simply of his friend, his family, or his tribe. He fights the fundamental forms of evil and harm, the descendants of the life-destroyer Cain—Grendel and his mother, envious of all human joy—and then the fire dragon, full of anger against man. He ostensibly avenges the harm done to the Danes in the one case and to his own Geats in the other, but the forms against which the vengeance flows out are mythical shorthand for what hurts all of us; they are not human enemies (as they are in most Germanic narratives) whose destruction might involve him in self-defeat or, as we say, in guilt. In other senses as well Beowulf is the one man in the poem who will *not* provoke the evils with which we hurt ourselves. He is the one who is not disloyal to his king, not treacherous towards his king's wife and son upon the king's demise, not ungenerous and murderous when he is a king himself, not cowardly—all things which others are guilty of in some dimension of the poem's curious allusiveness.

What is just as important, however, is that beyond all this he is not the bringer of a millenium, either, nor can anyone be, in the universe of the poem. The insistence upon the hero's ultimate overthrow is one of the work's most valuable heritages from the body of Germanic narrative. Beowulf resists evil for a time, but what hurts us, finally kills him as he is in the act of killing one of its forms. The two peoples whom he has principally benefited are both to be destroyed by their folly and others' vengeance. The ethical life of the poem, then, depends upon the propositions that evil can sometimes be truly identified, that those who fight it are good and those who conquer forms of it are wonderful, but that finally the evil that is part of this life is too much for the preeminent man, as it is for all the rest of us. The object of our vengeance is to destroy what hurts all of us, not to perpetuate more that is hurtful; but, justly maintaining that after all our efforts doom is there for all of us, the *Beowulf* is enabled to capitalize on the mighty pessimism of Germanic story.

The transmutation of Germanic mores from personal vengeance to the fight against evil depends partly on the Christianity of the author (see below), but the ethical views expressed above can be taken very seriously by many people today, whatever their religious belief, so that *Beowulf* remains morally very much alive. Two other dangers for the life of the poem, however, proceed from the author's method of embodying these notions in his poem. These are what usually bother the modern reader on first contact. They are elementary matters, but they must be defined in a somewhat roundabout way.

Readers in this century are accustomed to one kind of literary discourse, and one way of looking at the world through fiction, which might be called literary or moral realism. We tend to read fictional narratives from whatever culture in terms of this standard, which is usually first absorbed from novels and other fiction of the last two hundred years. What makes Homer's Achilles delightful to many of us is that, in spite of his millenial distance from us, he is immediately believable because he is a mixture of qualities—a supreme fighter, but childishly uncooperative and sulky; utterly vengeful and then, suddenly, amenable to fellow-feeling for his enemy Priam and to a sense of the total human plight. Contrariwise, in similar fictional situations we have learned from modern literature to recognize a completely good or bad character as unsatisfactory. He is a dishonest creation because no one is "really" like that, and he is a nonfunctioning inhabitant of his fictional world because his creator has not employed the chief resource of the modern imagination: the sense of the complexity, the "liveliness" of life. A contemporary reader often has a very good nose for this feature of a bad novel. Such a reader is likely to apply the standards of realistic fiction to *Beowulf* and to conclude that its hero is an incredible superman, or that he is as little revelatory of the true springs of human conduct as is the story of George Washington and the cherry tree. The two objections are, then, (1) that the *Beowulf* author is dishonest, or a dupe of his primitive milieu, in foisting upon us a figure of a kind which we shall never meet in our waking life, and (2) that the poem has no life to it because its main figures are puppets—Beowulf all light; Grendel, the latter's mother, and the dragon all in darkness. To put it another way, many who read *Beowulf* for the first time find it difficult to come to terms with its narrative as such, even though they may be prepared to admit that the *Beowulf* poet removed the curse of blood-guilt by opposing his hero to the supernatural enemy rather than to human ones. Many modern readers, in fact, would prefer not to admit even that, but to think that the author was too primitive in his thinking to have any choice in the matter, a harsh opposition between a perfect hero and an evil dragon or the like being the only fictional formula imaginable in those crude days. (This, by the way, is quite untrue; the background of the poem is full of the alternative formula of heroes face to face in dubious battle.)

In any case, the two difficulties are finally easy to understand because they are so elementary. If the poem really suffers from them, it can be left to historical study, like the tenth-century Continental *Waltharius,* in which the Germanic heroes are of such thin cardboard that the story turns to farce. It can probably be shown, however, that these objections are irrelevant in the case of *Beowulf.*

Almost everyone touched by modern culture agrees today that an art is possible beyond realism, embodying our deepest subliminal urges and convictions, of the kind which has been embodied in myth and which appears to us in dreams. People agree to this, generally because they have been told it so often, but many of them must not understand what is really involved, because, along with what is remarkable, so much merely modish and shallow art has made its mark under the aegis of this proposition. The truth of the proposition itself, however, is not in doubt. The most important and widespread example in Western culture is probably the Mass. In one sense it is art, and drama; however, its moving effect on those for whom it is celebrated depends not upon realistic features but upon its wonderfully artful summoning up of feelings about willing self-immolation, the participants' unity in the self-immolator, and His exemplary chieftainship over them. It is unnecessary to cite examples from modern literature, drama, or art, or from myths provided by the anthropologists, for every reader will probably supply his own.

Beowulf's artistic embodiment is mainly of the sort described. It is only a subsidiary point that some realistic touches are in fact given to the hero (to call a man drunk to his face at the mead-bench, as Beowulf does, argues a heedless forthrightness that would have done credit to the historical Father of his Country in one of his tempers). The main point is that *Beowulf* mobilizes mythical feelings and creates a mythical picture of life in a supremely artful way. The artfulness is very important. A local myth about life and death, heroic self-sacrifice, and final defeat by the enemy of us all is simply material for the original believers and the anthropologist no matter how true it is to our subliminal experience, unless it has something else to validate it as an independent work of art. Theoretically, this "something else" may be the realistic treatment that we first spoke of. Probably, however, only the best modern historical novels succeed in following the canons of realism and in giving psychological and material particularity to mythical material; in being so treated, their myths perhaps become something else. Considerations of this kind of particularity and realism are only marginal in our poem. Its artfulness is largely a matter of structure and style.

STRUCTURE

Only an early Germanic audience would have come naturally by the kind of information that elucidates *Beowulf's* structure. We may take a particular example and then examine the whole structure of the poem summarily.

One of the apparently most confused sequences in *Beowulf* is what happens between the hero's defeat of Grendel (p. 39) and (on the next night) the fatal carrying off by Grendel's maddened mother of the beloved counselor Aeschere (p. 49). In the foreground of action there is no particular difficulty for the reader: the Danes and the Geatish visitors follow the wounded Grendel's spoor to the mere beneath which he has sunk; they return exulting to the hall; they feast; they retire; Grendel's mother comes and carries off Aeschere. But interlarded with all this, and taking up far more space, are the following: (1) during the return to the hall, a recitation of the deeds of the Germanic dragon-slayer Sigemund and a statement of how he and Beowulf differ from the evil king Heremod; (2) at the feast, a recitation of how a Danish princess named Hildeburh, having been married to Finn of the Frisians in order to establish peace with that people, had to see her Danish brother and her son murdered in a new outbreak between Danes and Frisians (later a Danish retainer murdered her husband in revenge, and she was taken back to Denmark); (3) at the feast, a speech in which Queen Wealhtheow of the Danes assures her relative Hrothulf that she looks forward with confident serenity to his helpful attitude towards her two sons after their father, King Hrothgar, will have died; (4) at the feast, a comparison of the treasures there bestowed on Beowulf with other treasures taken by one Hama, who underwent the envy of Ermanaric. Among Beowulf's treasures is a ring whose subsequent history is given (it passed to Beowulf's king, Hygelac; it was then lost in the battle with the Frisians when Hygelac was killed).

All of this sounds narratively confused—the kind of fiddling irrelevance which made earlier students of *Beowulf* believe that the work was an accretion of many hands, not the product of one author. But the situation is not really confused at all, if one knows what the author and his early audience knew. The first point to be held in mind is that the author is partly concerned with foreboding: at the feast just before they retire it is said of the guests, "They did not know the doom, grim destiny, which many of the nobles would meet." Then they go to bed and Grendel's mother carries off Aeschere to her den to eat him. Some sort of contrast between that and the joy of the feast is one of the things intended. What a contemporary audience would have been likely to know makes very good sense out of the apparent irrelevancies.

Wealhtheow, the queen, and her husband King Hrothgar had two sons and a daughter. After Hrothgar's passing, Hrothulf, instead of justifying Wealhtheow's expectations ("I am sure that . . . he will treat our sons well"), deposed and killed one of the sons and was in turn killed by the other, as we know from elsewhere. As to the daughter, Freawaru, we know that she has been be-

trothed to the chief of another tribe in order to end a feud; Beo-
wulf later predicts (p. 63) that the peace will not last, but that a
retainer of one side, inflamed to vengeance by a friend, will at-
tack the other. Her sorrow, in other words, and the situation be-
tween the two peoples, will strongly resemble the sorrow of that
other bereaved Danish princess, the wife of Finn, and the situa-
tion between the Danes and the Frisians as recited at the feast.
The future situation, in fact, will probably be worse. We judge
from another source that it is the tribe of Freawaru's husband
which will eventually burn down Heorot, the very hall in which
this feast is given. That will be the end of the Danes. Further-
more, the future of the ring which is presented to Beowulf
(Wealhtheow says to Hrothgar, "Rejoice . . . . Be gracious to the
Geats, remembering how many gifts you have gathered from far
and near") is an earnest of "grim destiny": Beowulf's king, wear-
ing it, loses everything, life included, in the disastrous battle of
his Geats with the Frisians.

Not all of the significances here are so bitter: Hrothulf stands
in contrast to Beowulf, who after the death of his own king pro-
tects the heir and the queen instead of usurping the kingdom as
he could easily have done; perhaps Ermanaric stands in the same
relation to Beowulf, for he is a type of the evil ruler in this poem
and elsewhere. The story of Sigemund the dragon slayer, how-
ever, which in the action constitutes simply praise of Beowulf for
destroying Grendel, has darker tones: Sigemund ventures beneath
a stone to kill a dragon; so, later, will Beowulf venture. But Sig-
emund's dragon guards a treasure having a death-curse for him
who takes it, and Beowulf's slaying of the treasure-guarding drag-
on will be at the expense of his own life; that treasure, too, is ac-
cursed. The song in praise of Beowulf's victory, then, is an antici-
pation of his own end.

It follows from all that has been said, therefore, that the series
of apparently wandering interruptions in the action between the
death of Grendel and the carrying off of Aeschere are repeated
reminders to the general tune of "They did not know the doom,
grim destiny, which many of the nobles would meet": feasting
and joyful, the hall companions do not imagine that the enemy
from the outer darkness will immediately renew the assault and
carry off one most important among them; in a larger sense, the

elated actors in the drama do not realize that the Danes are to undergo later repeated blows of fate, that the hero will be destroyed, and, in fact, that his destruction will signify the beginning of the end for his tribe, the Geats. In the largest sense of all, an elegiac view of life is powerfully generated. The mood, if not the substance, is the same as in the story quoted by the Old English writer Bede in his *Ecclesiastical History of the English People:* man's life is like the flight of a bird, which, buffeted by a storm, flies into a bright hall where men are feasting, and then flies directly through an opposite window into the darkness again.

The author seems to follow this method throughout. Story, brief allusion, or event looks backward and forward or at the human lot so as to give a strong emotional direction to any particular part of the narrative and to tie the whole together in extremely complex ways. One need not fear the complexity, however, since the method resembles the associative ones in a number of modern authors who depend on our common stock of knowledge for the raw material of their effects. A reference to George Washington and the cherry tree would not be illuminating to an Old English audience but is to us; and a modern poet who, desiring to create a sinister effect in connection with these associations, followed on with the Washington Tidal Basin, gifts from the Japanese, and Pearl Harbor, would probably impress the *Beowulf* poet as very subtle after the progression of ideas had been explained to him. While the reader of a translation cannot fully appreciate the powerful atmospheric quality of the style in rendering these allusions forceful, he can nevertheless see for himself how the structure of the poem directs thought and feeling into deep channels. The original audience would probably have seen the poet's points immediately. From parallel references in the *Beowulf* itself, in the Old English poems *Deor, Widsith,* and *Finnsburh,* in the material of the Icelandic Edda and sagas, and in the *Nibelungenlied,* we know that many of our poet's allusions were to a common stock of stories and heroes known throughout the Germanic world.

Having considered one sequence in detail, we pass on now to a summary examination of the total structure of *Beowulf.*

We have a funeral at each end of the poem. *Beowulf* opens

with the mysterious arrival from the sea of the culture hero of the Danes. His name, Scyld Scefing, is given to them ("Scyldings" is a modernized equivalent of a word often used for the Danes in the Old English original); "Scefing" may suggest a sheaf of wheat—in which case he is a fertility figure as well. His funeral ship bears him out to sea, again mysteriously; certainly it looks forward to the funeral pyre of Beowulf, that other benefactor of peoples, upon a headland at the conclusion. The poem falls into two parts: the hero's exploits in youth as a generous helper of the Danes, and his adventure in age in benefiting his own tribe in Sweden. But the first part looks forward to the misfortunes of the Danes—the dissension and sorrows of the rulers, the final destruction of their great hall Heorot by flame, as already suggested. The first part also conveys, in its allusions to the behavior of Unferth and Hrothulf, the counterpoint of misdemeanor against which Beowulf stands out. And, most powerfully in the lay sung in celebration of his first victory, but also elsewhere, it suggests his final defeat and the general elegiac bent of the work. Throughout, the behavior of evil rulers like Heremod contrasts pointedly with the actions of Beowulf, the later king. Between the first and second parts falls the great speech of the aged Danish king, Hrothgar. It is rich in pronouncements. His prescriptions for manhood and kingship look backward into history and forward into the career of Beowulf; his prohibitions are similarly allusive; and his statement of the common fate looks forward to Beowulf's end and the ensuing, predicted doom. In the second part symmetry is given to Beowulf's career by his slaying of the dragon, but the victory, in the descending arc of life, is ideally sacrificial: he gives his life for his people.

The suggestions of ruin here are overpowering. The dragon is guarding the treasure of a vanished race; we hear the lament of its last member. We realize that the end of Beowulf's race is also in view. The pattern of loyalty, always firmly held by the hero himself, is broken. Of twelve chosen warriors only one, the virtuous Wiglaf, helps Beowulf in his final need. The vultures of tribal vengeance will now come home to roost: the Frisians whom the Geats had attacked under Hygelac will attack the Geats; the tribe will now be defenseless before the onslaught of the neighboring Swedes, with whom there is an enduring feud. The horrible inevitability of thrust and counterthrust in these patterns of loyalty and vengeance comes home to us as to the original audience of Germanic story only if we are allowed to stand and count the bloodthirsty blows as the author enumerates them: Haethcyn, brother of Hygelac of the Danes, had captured the wife of Ongentheow, king of the Swedes; Ongentheow and his band had then killed Haethcyn. Hygelac attacked Ongentheow, and Eofor, a member of the Geatish band, killed Ongentheow; Hygelac gave his daughter to Eofor as a reward. Ongentheow's son Onela was now on the Swedish throne. His brother's sons, Eanmund and Eadgils, exiled for rebellion, were befriended by Hygelac's son Heardred, who had succeeded to the Danish throne after Hygelac's death among the Frisians. Onela attacked and killed Heardred. Beowulf, now king, inherited the feud and helped Eadgils, who, thus aided, killed Onela and became king of the Swedes.

There is at the time of Beowulf's death further rich cause for mutual extermination. Eanmund, the brother of Eadgils, had been killed by one Weohstan, a retainer of Onela. Who, from the present Swedish king Eadgils' point of view, inherits the blood-guilt from Weohstan? None other than Weohstan's son Wiglaf, the loyal young warrior of the dragon fight, who is now to be king of the Geats. As usual with the *Beowulf* author, this final calamity is hinted at, not expressed baldly; and the general parallel between it and the troubles of the Danes is also left for the reader to guess.

STYLE

The main tradition of Germanic verse was oral. A professional, called a *scop*, spoke or chanted narrative verses on festive occasions, as happens in the narrative of *Beowulf*. As noted, his chanting was probably accompanied by the sound of a harp (see p. 5). This may have been plucked only occasionally, to help out the meter; exactly how it was used is unclear. A number of habitual phrases—bardic formulae—made it possible for him to improvise rapidly, in the way of folk minstrels in other oral poetic traditions. For instance, the phrase *theod-cyningas* ("people-kings," "kings of the nation") is often used in place of mere *cyningas* because it fills up a half-line exactly, not because of a necessary distinction from other kinds of kings. As is pointed out by F. P. Magoun,[2] the first investigator of this important class of devices in Old English, metrically similar variations of *theod-cyningas* are often improvised, for the same reason: *cyninga* may be prefixed by *eorth-* ("earth-kings"), *heah-* ("high kings"), *sae-* ("sea-kings"), and other expressions.

Undoubtedly some of the Old English poems that have come down to us were composed by persons who were not in the first place *scops,* but men of the church, or at least men who had received a religious education. No doubt they sometimes wrote down their poems instead of reciting them, but they continued to use the traditional style, the formulae, and the versification of the originally unlettered, speaking or chanting, professional bards. We are not sure to what class the *Beowulf* poet belonged, but it is almost inconceivable that he was not literate, in fact well educated. He may, for instance, have borrowed some of his descriptive matter from Vergil's *Aeneid,* although of this we are not at all sure. Since *Beowulf* is so sophisticated and integrated a poem, there is a tendency to believe that it was composed, so to speak, in writing. Undoubtedly, however, most of those who knew it in Old English times heard it rather than read it.

What all this means for style is that, however literate its author was, we must think of his words as intended for the ear, not the eye. In the poem repetition reinforces the understanding, and habitual phrases and epithets are part of the tradition. Perhaps the chief qualities of his style are dignity, amplitude, and lyricism. He, and all in his tradition, understood the distance and otherness which the lofty phrase lends to events. A just appreciation of the solemnity and importance of epic happenings is implicit in the treasured repetitions of his style. He is not being tiresome, but is communicating to an audience the heroic grandeur of his

---

[2] "The Oral-Formulaic Character of Anglo-Saxon Narrative Poetry," republished in *An Anthology of Beowulf Criticism,* ed. L. E. Nicholson (University of Notre Dame Press, 1963), p. 198.

subject when he says in three different ways that Beowulf killed the dragon, or even that Hrothgar went to bed. These acts are noble. They are not like ours. Each dignified reiteration of the event can be received with something like a thrill of pleasure if one realizes the choiceness of the precious subject. Thus the dignity and the amplitude.

Because *Beowulf* is so much a poem of directed emotion, and so little, comparatively, of direct narrative, its style must also be lyrical. The readjustment of the mood by the addition of an extra epithet, and then yet another, the long passages of lament, or of expatiation on the particular grisliness of fen, moor, or water, hardly differ, to the layman's eye, from those in Old English lyrics like *The Seafarer* and *The Wanderer:* both are mood-poetry, atmospheric; and an experiencing of the gloomy word-painting of *Beowulf* is one of the greatest and most virile pleasures of reading the poem in the original. One would wish to say, if the phrase had not been cheapened, that the composition of *Beowulf* is musical rather than narrative—more like an organ being played than a series of events being told.

As in other Germanic poetry, the style of *Beowulf* is figurative. The *kenning,* a metaphorical device described for us by the medieval Icelander Snorri Sturluson, is fairly frequent: "swan-road" and "gannet-bath" are the sea; "sea-garment" is a sail. Most often these are habitual, not freely invented. They are generally so devious that to preserve them and to make sense to a modern reader are mutually incompatible aims in a translation. There are various allied expressions, all of them part of an honorific and exalted vocabulary of the kind which is common to epic narrative everywhere. "Unlock one's word-hoard" (say), the patronymic epithet, like "son of Ecgtheow" (Beowulf), and references to the raven of battle and the eagle and the wolf who devour the slain are all to be found in *Brunanburh* and *Judith* as well as *Beowulf.* Nearly the same expressions occur frequently in other Old English poems, but they are never used more appositely than by the *Beowulf* poet. It is very difficult for us, who find these expressions extremely picturesque, to divine how habitual or how striking they seemed originally in context.

Another frequent device in *Beowulf* and in other Old English poetry is understatement or negative affirmation—meiosis or litotes—which produces controlled and usually macabre humorous effect, as when one says after falling over a cliff that it was not on that occasion that one had felt true pleasure. Much of *Brunanburh* is a tissue of such figures. Something analogous in the way of subdued, savage irony emerges from such an habitual figure as that describing one party's reaction to the fact that Wiglaf's spirit and his sword did not weaken when he helped Beowulf in the final battle with the dragon: "The serpent found this out when they had come together." The reader needs to watch out for such expressions, because they are easy to glide over.

CHRISTIANITY AND PAGANISM

It has already been suggested that Christian influence had a part in the *Beowulf* poet's choice of supernaturally evil figures rather than men as Beowulf's enemies (although of course these figures belonged originally to the realm of folklore). In addition, however, there are a number of overtly Christian references in the body of the poem: to an Almighty who is just, to a shepherd who cares for souls and a malicious being who attacks them when they are not vigilant, to a power that helps those who help themselves. There are also definite Biblical reminiscences. Grendel is said to be descended from Cain; the sword hilt which Beowulf brings back to Hrothgar from the underwater battle with Grendel's mother has an inscription referring to an ancient race of giants, alien to God and flood-whelmed, reminiscent of the *Nephilim* or giants of Genesis vi. On the other hand, the frequent references to an inscrutable, all-controlling fate; to being fated, i.e., doomed to die; and to a man's fame as the only thing which will live after him are all in accord with what we know of Germanic pagan habits of thought, although there are no references to the ancient Germanic divinities.

It has been suggested that all or some of the Christian references are simply a confused amalgam of imperfectly understood Christianity and residual paganism. Our understanding of this matter is still unsatisfactory, but there is another tenable theory. Notions of an agency (loosely, fate or fortune) which, under the ultimate control of the Godhead, yet seems to us to control our lives inscrutably and arbitrarily, are not alien to the most sophisticated Christian thinking; consequently the *Beowulf* poet's similar references may be totally in accord with Christian principles. As far as fame is concerned, it is easy to show that poets even of the time of Shakespeare sometimes made use of the idea of an "eternity of fame" as though after death a man's reputation was the most important residuum. We all now believe, as well, that certain other works around our poet's time avoided all references to Christianity and yet were written by Christians in accordance with Christian notions. *The Consolation of Philosophy* (sixth century) is the chief example.

In fact, a reading of other Old English poems may lead to the conviction that the puzzle about whether the Christian references in *Beowulf* are, or are not, later interpolations is not a real one. *Deor, The Dream of the Rood,* and *Maldon* contain both Christian elements and remnants of pagan thinking, but no reader would suppose that either the Christian references or the pagan ones in these short poems are interpolations. The amalgam of traditions is in the mind of a single author in each case; it is not a result of accretions by successive authors.

OTHER CONSIDERATIONS

Many matters in *Beowulf* have a fairly sure historical basis. Hygelac's battle in Frisian territory occurred about A.D. 521. The Danes, Swedes, and Geats of the time are known to history. Hrothgar and Hrothulf are discussed in a twelfth-century chronicle. The site of Heorot has been located fairly reliably in a village near Roskilde, on the same island as Copenhagen. The burial mounds of Ongentheow and Ohthere in Sweden are known.

Legendary references or parallels to matters that come up in *Beowulf* exist in fair number in the Old English poems *Widsith* and *Deor,* in sagas (particularly *The Saga of Hrolf Kraki* and

The Saga of Grettir), and elsewhere. Surprisingly, no references to a hero named Beowulf have come down to us, except for the poem itself.

The probable date and place of composition have already been touched on. If the praise which the poet gives, in the first banquet scene, to one Offa as the husband of Thryth (?) could be shown to be a compliment to Offa's descendant of the same name who was a famous Mercian king of the later eighth century, we should have stronger reasons for believing that *Beowulf* was written at the latter's court and in his time. Linguistic evidence indicates either a Mercian or a Northumbrian origin and points towards an earlier date, the first half of the eighth century. Our text in the apparently tenth-century manuscript shows traces of a number of different dialects: it must therefore be a copy at a number of removes from the original. Scribes of some of the earlier successive copies, themselves speaking different dialects, probably substituted word forms of their own, somewhat different from those in the original.

The most startling archaeological find in England in recent times is the Sutton Hoo ship, found in Suffolk, near Ipswich, in 1939. In the seventh century it had been lowered into an excavation, had been partly filled with treasure, and had been covered with a mound, probably in connection with the funeral ceremonies of a king. The objects found there come up fully to the standard suggested by Scyld Scefing's funeral ship, and are of a sumptuousness and technical excellence not previously dreamed of as possible in Anglo-Saxon times. Of particular interest to readers of *Beowulf* are an ornate helmet; a sword with a remarkable inlaid pommel; a great gold buckle of intricate design; many pieces of cloisonné work in gold and garnet with spectacular patterns of great precision; the remains of a shield having among other inlays a magnificent gold dragon; a harp; and what appears to be a battle standard. Many other things were found in the ship, some suggesting a cosmopolitan culture: a great silver dish comes from the eastern Mediterranean. Like the manuscript of the poem, all these objects are housed in the British Museum in London. They are well worth seeing.

                                                          A. K. H.

⊰ BEOWULF ⊱

*The ancestry of Hrothgar, King of Denmark,
and the building of the great hall Heorot*

Indeed, we have heard of the great Danish kings in days of old and the noble deeds of the princes. Scyld Scefing[1] often drove troops of enemies from their mead-hall seats; he terrified the lords of many tribes, although he had once been a destitute foundling. He found consolation for that: he prospered under the heavens, and grew in glory, until every one of his neighbors over the sea had to obey him and pay tribute. He was a good king.

Then a son was born to him, a child in the house, sent by God to help the people—He saw the distress they had suffered before when they were without a ruler for a long time. Therefore the Lord of Life, Ruler of Heaven, granted worldly honor to the son of Scyld. Beowulf[2] was famous; his renown spread far and wide in the land of the Danes. A young man should do as he did, and

---

[1] Mythical ancestor of the Danish kings. His mysterious arrival and equally mysterious "passing" suggest divine origin; his name suggests both his function as king (shield—protector of the people), and, possibly, a nature myth ("son of a sheaf," or "child with a sheaf").

[2] (I) Danish king, son of Scyld Scefing and grandfather of Hrothgar; not to be confused with Beowulf (II), hero of the poem—who is not even related to the Danish royal house.

23

with splendid gifts from his father's store win loyal companions who will stand by him in old age and serve the people when war comes. He who does praiseworthy deeds will prosper everywhere.

Scyld departed from him at the fated time: the strong one went into the keeping of the Lord. His own dear retainers bore away the beloved king who had governed them so long to the current of the sea, as he himself had ordered while he could still use words. There in the harbor stood a ring-prowed ship, covered with ice and ready to set out; it was a craft fit for a prince. They laid their dear lord, the giver of rings, in the bosom of the ship; they put the glorious one by the mast. Many treasures and precious things from far away were brought there—never was a ship more beautifully equipped with armor and weapons of war, swords and coats of mail. On the dead lord's bosom lay a multitude of treasures that were to go far with him in the power of the flood; nor did they give him less valuable treasure than did those who first sent him forth, alone over the waves, when he was a child. They set a golden banner high over his head; then they gave him to the sea and let the water carry him away. Their spirits were saddened, their hearts mournful. No man, not even the wisest counselor in the world, could say with certainty who received that cargo.

When the prince his father was gone, Beowulf, son of Scyld, reigned over the people; he was renowned among nations for a long time. To him in turn was born noble Healfdene, who ruled the Danes gloriously as long as he lived—a venerable leader, fierce in battle. To Healfdene, the leader of hosts, four children all told were born into the world: Heorogar and Hrothgar and Halga the Good, and a daughter, who, they say, was Onela's[3] queen—consort of the Swedish king.

Then Hrothgar was granted success in battle and glory in war, so that his friends and kinsmen obeyed him willingly, and his band of warriors grew large. It came into his mind to order a great mead-hall to be built, larger than the children of men had ever heard of; within it he would give out all that God gave him (except the public land and the lives of men) to young and old.

---

[3] King of Sweden (see genealogical tables). He killed Heardred, king of the Geats, and was later killed by his rebellious nephew, Eadgils.

He ordered work to adorn the building from nations far and wide throughout this earth. The time soon came when the greatest of halls was quite ready, and the ruler gave it the name of Heorot. He did not forget his promise to give out rings and treasures at the feast. The hall towered, high and wide-gabled: it awaited the hostile flames of hateful fire. The time had not yet come when deadly hate would arise between a son and father-in-law after a deed of violence.

PART I: The Cleansing of Heorot

1. Grendel (lines 86–193)

An accursed monster terrorizes the Danish court for twelve years

This was an evil time for a certain powerful demon. He who dwelt in darkness heard loud rejoicing in the hall every day. There was the sound of the harp and the sweet song of the minstrel, who told about the creation of men, long ago; he said that the Almighty made the earth, the beautiful land bounded by the water; then, triumphant, He placed the sun and the moon as a light to lighten those who dwell on the land, and adorned the earth with branches and leaves; and He also created every living creature which moves after its kind. —Thus the retainers of Hrothgar lived in joy and happiness, until the hellish fiend began his wicked deeds.

This grim spirit was called Grendel. A notorious prowler of the waste lands, he held sway in the moors, the fen and fastness. The miserable creature had long inhabited the haunts of monsters, since the Creator had condemned him and all his race, the progeny of Cain,[4] in vengeance for the slaying of Abel. Cain got no joy by his murderous act, but was banished by the Eternal Lord; God drove him from mankind for that crime, and from him were descended all evil broods—ogres, elves and monsters,

---

[4] The Biblical first murderer; see Genesis 4: 1–15.

and those giants who long contended against God: He paid them back for that!

When night fell, Grendel went to inspect the great house; he came to see how the Danes had settled down after drinking beer. There he found the band of warriors sleeping after the feast, unconscious of sorrow and the misery of mankind. The evil creature was alert at once; the cruel and savage monster took thirty thanes in their beds. Exulting in his booty, he went back to seek out his home with his fill of slaughter.

The gray of dawn made Grendel's might in war apparent to all. Where there had been mirth, there was weeping, a great cry in the morning.

The glorious chief sat joyless; the prince, mighty of old, endured sorrow for his thanes when they saw the track of the foe, the accursed demon. The trouble now was severe beyond measure, hateful and long lasting: there was no further respite, but again the next night he committed more murder—he did not shrink from hostile act and wicked deed, for he was too fixed in the fetters of sin. Now it was easy to find a man who looked for a resting place further away, a bed in other buildings, when he had seen a clear sign of the invader's hatred: now he who escaped the enemy kept himself further away in a safer place.

The monster prevailed in this way and contended against right, one against all, until the best of houses stood empty. That lasted a long time: for twelve winters the Danish lord was afflicted with these troubles and suffered great sorrow. Sad lays made it openly known to men that Grendel warred against Hrothgar for a long time; he waged warfare, committed wicked deeds and hostile acts, for many seasons of continual strife. He did not want peace with any of the Danish host; he did not wish to stop his deadly evil, nor to settle the feud with payment—none of the counselors had reason to expect great compensation from the hand of the murderer. On the contrary, the dark death-shadow persecuted young and old, lingered and ambushed. He held the misty moors in perpetual darkness—no man knows where such demons go.

Thus the enemy of mankind, the fearful outcast, often did many wicked deeds and perpetrated grievous injuries. In the dark nights he prowled Heorot, the richly decorated hall; but he could not approach the throne, the seat where treasure was given —God prevented him—nor feel gratitude for gifts.

All this was heartbreaking distress to the lord of the Danes. Many men of high rank sat down in frequent consultation as to what should be done, deliberating what would be best for brave men to do against the awful horror. At times they made sacrifices to idols in heathen temples, entreating the devil to help them relieve the distress of the people. Such was their custom, the hope of heathens—their thoughts were on hell, for they did not know God, the Judge of Deeds; they neither knew the Lord God nor understood how to worship the Protector of the Heavens, the Ruler of Glories. Woe to him who, in cruel affliction, shall thrust his soul into the embrace of the fire—he shall know no comfort or change. Well shall it be for him who may go to the Lord after the day of death and ask for peace in the bosom of the Father!

So Healfdene's son brooded continually over the trouble of the time; nor could the wise prince turn that misery aside. The strife which had come upon the people was too hateful and enduring, a cruel, dire distress—the greatest of evils that come by night.

2. Beowulf's Arrival (lines 194–498)

Beowulf comes from the land of the Geats to fight Grendel; he is welcomed by Hrothgar

A brave man of the tribe of the Geats, a thane of Hygelac,[5] heard in his homeland of Grendel's deeds. He was the strongest and mightiest man alive, noble and stalwart. He ordered a good ship prepared for him, saying he wished to seek out the warrior king over the sea, since that glorious leader had need of men. Wise men did not blame him for this venture, although he was dear to them: they encouraged the brave man, and looked at the omens. The hero had chosen the keenest champions he could find among the Geatish people, and it was as one of fifteen that he led the way to the ship, a skilled seaman leading his band to the shore.

[5] Beowulf's uncle, king of the Geats (a tribe living in southern Sweden).

In good time the boat was on the waves, floating under the cliffs. Watchful men climbed the prow. The ocean streams eddied, sea washed against sand, as the men bore bright trappings and splendid armor into the ship. The men shoved out: the warriors launched the well-braced craft on the longed-for journey. Driven by the wind, the boat went over the billowy sea, foamy necked, like a bird, until in due time on the following day the curved prow had advanced so that the seafarers saw land; they sighted the shining sea cliffs, the steep banks of the shore, the broad headlands. The sea had been crossed and the voyage was at an end. Quickly the people of the Geats mounted on the land and moored the ship—their battle garments, shirts of mail, rattled— and thanked God that their voyage had been easy.

From the wall the Danish guard, whose duty it was to guard the sea cliffs, saw them bear bright shields and ready armor over the gangway: he was eager to know who these men were. Hrothgar's thane rode his horse to the shore, and, brandishing a mighty spear in his hand, he asked in formal words, "What sort of warriors are you, men in armor, who have come thus over the sea in your lofty ship? I have been coast guard here for a long time, and have held watch by the sea so that no enemy might land a force to do harm on the land of the Danes. Never have armed men come here more openly—yet you did not have leave from our warriors, or the agreement of kinsmen. Never have I seen a mightier nobleman in the world, a greater man in armor, than one among you: surely that is no mere hall retainer exalted with weapons—unless his countenance and peerless appearance belie him. Now I must know your lineage before you may go further here on Danish land. Men from afar, seafarers, now hear my plain thought: it would be best to be quick to say where you come from."

The chief answered him; the leader of the band said, "We are people of the Geatish nation, Hygelac's hearth companions. My father was a noble leader well known among nations; he was called Ecgtheow. He lived through many winters, and was an old man when he departed from this world. Wise men remember him well all over the earth. We come with friendly intentions to seek your lord, the son of Healfdene; be of good counsel to us!

We have a weighty errand to the glorious lord of the Danes—nor, I think, will there be anything secret about it. You know whether what we have heard is true: that an enemy—I know not who, a mysterious persecutor—shows his strange hostility among the Danes in the dark nights and works injury and slaughter in a terrible way. I may be able to give Hrothgar sincere good counsel as to how he, who is so good and wise, may overcome the fiend—if a change is ever to be, if a cure for these miserable afflictions is to come in its turn, and sorrows end. Otherwise, he will suffer trials and distress for ever after, as long as the best of houses remains in its lofty place."

The guard, a fearless officer, spoke as he sat there on his horse: "An acute warrior who has a clear mind should be a judge of both words and deeds. I understand that this band is friendly to the lord of the Danes. Go on with your weapons and armor; I will guide you. Also, I shall bid my men to guard your boat honorably against every enemy, watch over the newly tarred vessel on the sand, until the curved-prowed ship again bears its beloved lord over the sea to the land of the Geats. One who does brave deeds will be allowed to survive the storm of battle unhurt."

They went on their way. The ship remained; the spacious vessel was moored with a rope, fast at anchor. Over the warriors' cheek-guards shone boar figures, decorated with gold, shining and hardened by fire: the warlike boar kept guard over the fierce ones. The company hastened until they could perceive the timbered hall, splendid and decorated with gold; that was the most famous building in the world, the dwelling of the mighty lord; its light shone over many lands. The guard showed them that bright home of brave men so that they could go straight to it, then turned his horse and said, "It is time for me to go. May the Almighty Father, by His grace, keep you safe in your undertaking! I shall go to the sea to keep watch against hostile bands."

The band of men followed along the pathway, over the street paved with stones. Their strong mail gleamed and the bright iron rings sang in their armor as they came to the hall in their warlike gear. Weary of the sea, they set their broad, strong shields against the wall of the building and sat down on the bench, with a ringing of chain mail. Their spears, war gear of seamen, stood gathered together, the ashwood gleaming gray at the tip; the band was well equipped with weapons.

There a noble champion asked the warriors of their descent: "From where have you brought decorated shields, gray coats of mail and visored helmets, a host of spears? I am Hrothgar's herald and officer. Never have I seen a bolder band of strangers. I think you have come to Hrothgar in daring mood: not as exiles seeking a refuge, but as bold-hearted men in search of adventure."

The famed hero answered him; the bold leader of the Geats rejoined, "We are Hygelac's table companions—Beowulf is my name. I wish to tell my errand to the son of Healfdene, the glorious prince who is your lord, if he who is so great will allow us to greet him." Wulfgar replied (he was a prince of the Wendels,[6] well known for his wisdom and valor): "I will ask the lord and ruler of the Danes, the giver of rings, as you request. I shall tell the glorious lord of your venture and quickly bring you back the answer the great one thinks fit to give me."

Quickly he turned to the place where Hrothgar, old and gray, sat with his band of nobles; the valiant warrior went up and stood by the shoulder of the Danish lord—he knew the custom of the court. Wulfgar spoke to his lord: "Geatish people are here, come from over the expanse of the water; the warriors call their chief Beowulf. My lord, they ask to exchange words with you. Do not refuse them your answer, gracious Hrothgar! They are well-armed men who seem worthy of the respect of nobles; and the chief who led these warriors here is certainly a powerful man."

Hrothgar answered, "I knew him when he was a boy. His father was called Ecgtheow; to him Hrethel,[7] king of the Geats, gave his only daughter in marriage. Now his bold son has come here to visit a good friend. The seafarers who have carried pleasant gifts to the Geats said that this famous warrior has the strength of thirty men in his grip. I expect that Holy God in His grace has sent him to the Danes to help us against Grendel's ter-

---

[6] Possibly the Vandels; very likely, the inhabitants of Vendel, in Sweden, or Vendill, in Jutland.
[7] A king of the Geats, father of Hygelac and grandfather of Beowulf (see genealogical tables).

ror. I shall offer the hero treasures for his daring. Hurry: bid the band of kinsmen to come in to see me and tell them that to the Danish people they are welcome."

Wulfgar hurried to the door and brought his message from within: "My victorious lord, the ruler of Denmark, bids me say to you that he knows of your noble descent and that you courageous men from over the sea are welcome to him. Now go in your battle gear, wearing your helmets, to see Hrothgar; let the shields and wooden spears remain here to await the result of the conference."

The hero arose with many a warrior around him: a troop of mighty thanes. Some stayed there to guard the war gear, as their leader ordered them, while the others hastened under Heorot's roof, the herald guiding them. The helmeted leader went on until he stood on the hearth.

His mail, the battle net linked by the skill of the smith, shone as Beowulf spoke: "Hail, Hrothgar! I am Hygelac's kinsman and retainer, and I have undertaken many a glorious deed in my youth. In my native land I heard of Grendel's doings. Seafarers say that this hall, the best of buildings, stands idle and useless to all when the evening light fades under heaven's vault.

"The noblest and wisest counselors of my people advised me to come to you, lord Hrothgar, because they knew of my great strength. They themselves saw me when, bloodstained from encounters with enemies, I came from battles, when I bound five giants and destroyed their race, and killed water monsters on the waves at night; I endured great hardship to avenge their persecution of the Geats—they had asked for trouble! I ground down those fierce creatures, and now I will fight against the monster Grendel; I alone shall settle the dispute with the demon.

"Chief of the Danes, protector of the nation, I want to ask one boon of you now—do not refuse me, defender of warriors and friend of the people, now that I have come so far—that I alone, with my bold troop of nobles, may purge Heorot.

"Also, I have learned that the monster, in his recklessness, does not care to use weapons; then, so that Hygelac, my lord, may rejoice over me in his heart, I will scorn to bear a sword or broad shield to the battle but will grapple against the fiend with my hands and fight for my life, enemy against enemy; he who is taken by death there must trust to God's judgment. I expect that if he can manage it he will devour the Geatish people in the battle hall without hesitation—to treat the host of the Geats as he often did others.

"If death takes me, there will be no need for you to cover my head, for Grendel will have my bloodstained body; he will bear off the bloody corpse to devour it. The solitary monster will eat ruthlessly, staining his moor retreat—and you will not have to worry longer over the disposal of my body. If I fall in battle, send Hygelac this best of war garments, finest of mail, which protects my breast; it is an heirloom of Hrethel, the work of Weland[8] the smith. Fate always does as she wills!"

Hrothgar replied: "You have come to us to fight in our defense and help us, my friend Beowulf. Your father's fighting brought about a great feud; he killed Heatholaf, among the Wylfings, so that the people of the Geats, fearing that war would result, could not help him. From there he came over the rolling waves to visit the Danish nation, when I first reigned over Denmark, and held the gracious realm, treasure city of warriors, in my youth. Heorogar was dead then—my elder brother was no longer living; he was a better man than I! After that I settled the feud with money. I sent ancient treasure over the water to the Wylfings; in return, Ecgtheow swore oaths to me.

"It is with great sorrow in my heart that I tell any man what Grendel has done to me in his malice—what injuries and calamities he has brought about in Heorot. My troop of retainers has grown smaller; Fate has swept my warriors off with Grendel's terror. God can easily put an end to the deeds of the mad ravager! Often warriors drunk with beer have vowed over the ale cup to wait in the beer hall with their swords for Grendel's onslaught. Then in the morning, when day broke, this mead-hall was bloodstained; all the bench planks were soaked with blood, the hall stained with battle gore. I had the fewer loyal men, beloved veteran retainers, since death had carried them off.

"—Now sit down to the banquet and speak your mind; tell men of your glorious victories, as your heart prompts."

[8] A legendary Germanic smith; his name was a guarantee of excellent workmanship.

A bench in the beer hall was yielded to the men of the Geats, and the brave champions went to sit there. A servant did his duty; bearing a decorated ale cup in his hands, he poured out the bright drink. From time to time a clear-voiced minstrel sang in Heorot, and the large company of warriors, Danes and Geats, rejoiced together.

3. Unferth Speaks of Breca (lines 499–670)

At the banquet table, Beowulf is challenged to explain an episode in his youth

Then Unferth, son of Ecglaf, spoke; sitting at the feat of the Danish lord, he began to quarrel; the undertaking of Beowulf, the brave seafarer, was a source of great chagrin to him because he did not want any other man on earth to win more glory in the world than he himself. "Are you that Beowulf who contested against Breca swimming on the wide sea, where you two in your pride dared the waters and ventured your lives because of foolish boasting? No one, neither friend nor enemy, could dissuade you two from that sorry undertaking when you swam in the sea; there you embraced the ocean stream, traveled over the paths of the sea with swinging hands, glided over the water. The ocean swelled in waves, in a winter flood.

"You both labored seven nights in the power of the water, but he had more might, and surpassed you in swimming. Then in the morning the sea carried him up on Norwegian land; from there he sought his own native country, the dear land of the Brondings, and there he governed the people, stronghold and treasure. Indeed, the son of Beanstan carried out his boast against you. Therefore, although you have always proved strong in the storm of battle, in grim war, I expect the worse results from you if you dare to wait for Grendel all night long."

Beowulf answered, "Well, my friend Unferth, drunk with beer, you have said a great many things about Breca and described his venture. I say this is the truth: that I had more strength in the sea, in struggling with the waves, than any other man. We two being young men still in the time of early youth, agreed and vowed that we would hazard our lives out on the sea, and we carried it out in this way.

"When we swam in the sea we each had a naked sword firmly in hand to defend ourselves against whales. He could not outdistance me, swimming more quickly in the sea, nor did I have any desire to go far from him. Thus we were together in the water for a period of five nights, until the flood drove us apart: the waters were welling, the weather most cold, and night darkening, and the north wind, grim as battle, turned against us; the waves were rough.

"The temper of the sea fishes was aroused. There my body armor, hard and strongly linked together, gave me help—the woven battle mail decorated with gold lay on my breast. A shimmering, deadly foe drew me to the bottom: the grim creature had me fast in his grip; however, I was able to pierce the monster with the point of my battle sword. The mighty sea beast was dispatched by my hand in the storm of battle. Thus the oppressors harrassed me constantly. I dealt with them with my good sword as they deserved—nor did the wicked destroyers of men have the pleasure of feasting on me, sitting around the banquet at the bottom of the sea.

"In the morning, they lay upon the shore wounded by the sword, put to sleep by the blade, so that they could never afterward hinder seafarers from making their way over the high seas. Light came from the east, God's bright beacon, and the water subsided, so that I could see the headlands of the sea, the windy walls. Fate often helps the undoomed man, when his valor is great! Thus it was my lot to slay nine sea monsters with the sword. I have never heard of a harder battle fought by night under the vault of heaven, nor of a man more distressed in the water; yet I survived that hostile grasp alive, though weary from the undertaking. Then the sea bore me off along the current of the flood; the welling water brought me onto the land of the Lapps.

"I have never heard any such perilous exploit told of you. Never yet did Breca, or you either, do such a bold deed in battle with your shining swords (although I do not think that one of my greater exploits), although you killed your brothers, your own close relatives; for that you will endure damnation in hell, no matter how clever you may be.

"I tell you the truth, son of Ecglaf: Grendel, that terrible monster, would never have done so many outrages in Heorot, such damage to your lord, if your heart and spirit were as warlike as you yourself say; he has discovered that he need not much dread the enmity of your people, the blades of the victorious Danes, so he takes his toll and shows mercy to none of the Danish nation, but enjoys himself, kills and harrasses, and does not expect battle from the Danes. But now I will soon show him the Geats' strength and courage in war. After that, whoever can do so will go boldly to the mead-hall when the morning light of another day, the sun clothed in radiance, shines from the south over the sons of men."

The generous king, gray haired and famous in battle, rejoiced at this. The prince of the glorious Danes expected help: the guardian of the people saw in Beowulf a mind firmly resolved.

Then there was much laughter of men, the pleasing sound of music and joyous words. Wealhtheow, Hrothgar's queen, came forward courteously; adorned with gold, she greeted the men in the hall. The noble wife first gave the cup to the Danish lord, bidding him to be blithe at the beer drinking, and the famous king gladly took his share of the feast and the cup. Then the Helming[9] lady went around to each group of retainers, young and old, giving the precious cups, until the time came when the clear-minded queen, adorned with rings, bore the mead cup to Beowulf. She greeted the leader of the Geats and thanked God in well-chosen words that this joy had come to her—that she expected the hero to give them relief from attacks.

The fierce warrior received the cup from Wealhtheow, and, ready for battle, he said: "When I set out on the sea and embarked in that boat with my band of men, I resolved that I would certainly do the will of your people—or else fall in the field of battle, fast in the grip of the foe. I shall do great deeds of valor, or else meet my death in this mead-hall!"

[9] Wealhtheow's family.

These words, the vow of the Geat, pleased the lady well. The noble, ring-adorned queen went to sit by her lord. Once again, as before, brave words were spoken in the hall; the people rejoiced and the sound of conquerors was heard, until presently the son of Healfdene wished to go to his evening rest—he knew that the monster had planned an attack on the high hall all day, from the time when they first saw the light of the sun until the darkening night with dusky shades came moving over all, black under the clouds.

All the band arose. Hrothgar saluted Beowulf and wished him good luck and control of the wine hall, saying, "Never before, while I could lift hand and shield, have I given over the splendid hall of the Danes to any man, until now to you. Now guard and keep the best of houses; consider your glory, show your mighty valor, and watch against the enemy. You shall not lack for good things if you survive this valorous work with your life."

Then Hrothgar left them; the Danish prince went out of the hall with his band of warriors. The chieftain wished to seek his bedfellow, Wealhtheow, the queen. The most Glorious of Kings had, men said, set a guard against Grendel—one who performed a special service for the lord of the Danes and offered a watch against the giant. Indeed, the chief of the Geats eagerly trusted in his own courage and might, and the grace of God.

4. The Fight with Grendel (lines 671–836)

How Beowulf overcame the monster with his bare hands

Now Beowulf took off his iron mail and the helmet from his head. He gave his adorned sword, the most choice of steel weapons, to an attendant, and ordered him to guard the battle gear. Before he climbed into bed the brave Geat spoke these proud words: "I do not consider myself a lesser fighter than Grendel does himself; therefore I will not kill him with a sword, and deprive him of life in that way—though I surely could. He does not know the proper ways to strike back at me and hew my shield in spite of the fact that he is renowned for hostile works. No: this night we two will abstain from swords, if he dares seek out a fight without weapon. Afterwards, may the wise God, the holy Lord, assign glory to whichever side seems fitting to Him."

Then the bold warrior lay down; his pillow received the hero's face, and around him many a bold seaman lay down on his bed in the hall. None of them thought that he would ever hereafter return to his beloved home, or see his people or the noble dwelling where he grew up, for they had heard that in the past murderous death had borne off all too many of the Danish people. But the Lord granted the destiny of success in war to the Geatish people; He gave them such comfort and help that they overcame their enemy, through the power and might of one man. It is truly said that mighty God has always ruled mankind.

In the dark night the one who walked in shadow came gliding. The warriors who were to guard that gabled house slept—all but one. Men knew that if God did not wish it the demon foe could not draw them down into the shades. But one watched against the foe in deadly rage, and angrily awaited the result of the battle.

Then Grendel came from the moor, moving under the misty hills. God's curse rested on him. The foe of men intended to ensnare some human being in the high hall. He advanced under the clouds to a place where he could easily recognize the wine hall of men, decorated with gold. That was not the first time he had visited Hrothgar's home—but never in all the days of his life, before or after, did he find thanes in the hall with worse results for himself! The joyless creature proceeded to the building.

The door, fastened as it was with forged bands, gave way at once when he touched it with his hands. Then the evil-minded creature, in his rage, tore open the entrance to the building and quickly trod on the handsome paved floor. The fiend's temper was aroused; from his eyes came an unlovely light, like a hellish flame. He saw many warriors in the building—the band of kinsmen sleeping together, a troop of young warriors—and his spirit exulted. The horrible monster intended to tear the life from the body of every one of them before day came. He hoped for his fill of feasting. But it was not destined that he would be able to partake of any more of mankind after that night.

Hygelac's nephew saw the evildoer go about his attack. The monster had no intention of delaying. Quickly he took, as his first step, a sleeping man—and eagerly tore him, bit into the body and drank the blood in streams, swallowed huge morsels; soon he had eaten all of the dead man, even his feet and hands. He moved along further and reached toward the hero where he lay in his bed: the fiend grasped at Beowulf, who rejoined savagely at once, rising up upon his arm.

Now the ghoul found that never in the world, anywhere on earth, had he met a man with a mightier handgrip. He became afraid in his heart, but he could not get away any the sooner. He was eager to be off; he wanted to flee to his hiding place and seek out the company of devils—his circumstances there were unlike any he had ever before encountered in all the days of his life. The brave man, Beowulf, remembered his vows of that evening: he stood upright and got a fast hold on the monster, with his fingers bursting; as the giant tried to turn away, the hero stepped further. However he could manage it, the infamous wretch meant to take flight to some place further away—to flee to his retreat in the fens. That journey to Heorot was a sorry one for the enemy! The mead-hall resounded so with the din that it brought terror to the Danes in their stronghold and alarmed all the brave warriors.

Both the fierce claimants to the building were enraged, and the hall resounded. It was a great wonder that the fair building withstood the clash of the warriors without falling to the ground, but it was firmly fastened in a skillful way, both inside and out, with iron bands. They say that many a mead-bench adorned with gold started from the floor where the angry foes struggled. Before that night no Dane had thought that any man could ever break up that excellent hall, adorned with antlers, by any means at all; they thought none had the skill to pull it asunder—unless it should be swallowed by flames, in the embrace of the fire.

Strange noise rose up again and again; a dreadful terror stirred the Danes and seized every man who heard through the wall the lamentation of God's adversary, singing his terrible dirge, his song of the defeat—the captive of hell wailing sorely, for he who was strongest and mightiest of living men held him fast.

The last thing the chief of heroes wished was to let the murderous intruder go alive; he did not consider Grendel's life to be useful to anyone. Now many of Beowulf's noble companions drew their ancient swords, wishing to defend the life of the lord, their glorious leader, in any way they could. The stouthearted warriors engaged in combat and tried to hew at the monster from every side, seeking his life, but what they did not know was that no sword could touch the evildoer, not even the choicest steel on earth: for he had cast a spell which made weapons useless, every blade!

But he was to make a miserable parting from life on that day; the alien spirit was destined to travel afar in the power of fiends. Now he who had afflicted the hearts of mankind so much in earlier days, and had committed so many crimes because he was feuding with God—he discovered that his body would not avail him: for Hygelac's brave kinsman had him by the hand.

Neither could bear to see the other remain alive. The horrible monster felt mortal pain as a great wound appeared on his shoulder; his sinews sprang open; the joint burst. Beowulf was granted glory in battle.

Mortally wounded, Grendel had to flee away into the fen slopes to seek his joyless dwelling. He knew all too well that his life had come to an end, that the number of his days had run out.

The wish of all the Danes had come to pass after the bloody conflict. That wise, brave man who had come from far away had purged Hrothgar's hall and saved it from violence. He rejoiced in the night's work, in his deeds of valor; the leader of the Geat warriors had carried out his vow to the Danes, and had so remedied all the grief and hard sorrow they had endured before, and had had to suffer out of dire necessity—no little affliction. The victory was evident to all when the brave warrior put the hand, arm, and shoulder under the vaulted roof: there was Grendel's grip, all together.

5. Joy in Heorot (lines 837–1008)

The Danes tell tales of other famous heroes as they rejoice over Beowulf's deed

They say that in the morning many warriors gathered in the hall. Leaders of the people came from near and far, through distant regions, to see the wonder and follow the tracks of the enemy. His parting from life did not sadden any of those who saw the vanquished creature's trail, and saw how, barely alive and weary in spirit when he had been overcome in battle, the doomed fugitive went on into the mere of the water demons. There the water boiled with blood: the terrible turmoil of the waves was mingled with hot gore, the blood of the battle surged. Doomed to death, Grendel lay concealed there until, deprived of all joys, he laid down his life and gave up his heathen soul in his fen refuge; hell received him there.

From there the veterans, together with many younger men, returned from the joyful journey, boldly riding their horses from the mere. Beowulf's glorious deed was spoken of, and many said over and over again that north or south, between the seas and over the wide earth, there was no better swordsman under the compass of the skies, nor one more worthy of rule. But, they did not find fault with their dear lord, gracious Hrothgar, at all; for he was a good king.

From time to time the warriors let their bay horses gallop, rivaling each other—the thoroughbreds raced along where the pathways seemed good. At times, one of the king's distinguished thanes, whose mind was full of lays and who remembered many old traditions, composed a new poem, in properly linked words. Skillfully he began to treat of Beowulf's venture, and successfully he uttered an apt tale, varying his words.

He told all he had heard about Sigemund's[10] deeds of valor—

---

[10] A great legendary Germanic hero; best known to us today through a different version used by Wagner in his operas (the "ring cycle"), in which Siegmund's son, Siegfried, is the dragon-slayer.

many strange things about his struggles and his travels far and wide, and feuds and treacheries. No one knew anything about these things except only Fitela—his uncle would speak of such things to his nephew when he wanted; for they were always comrades in arms at every battle and had slain a great many giants with their swords. Sigemund won no little fame after his deathday, when the strong warrior had killed the dragon who was guardian of a treasure hoard. Under the gray stone the prince's son dared the bold deed alone—not even Fitela was with him. Yet it turned out well for him, in that his sword went through the wondrous dragon until that splendid iron weapon stood still in the wall, and the dragon was slain. The hero's valor had brought it to pass that he might enjoy the ring hoard at his own will. Sigemund loaded a boat and bore bright treasure into the bosom of the ship; the dragon melted in its own heat.

He was famous among nations for his adventures, eminent among warriors for his couragous deeds; thus he prospered after Heremod's[11] glory faded and his strength and daring had diminished. Among the Jutes, Heremod was betrayed into the power of fiends; he was quickly put to death. Trouble upon trouble oppressed him too long—he was a great care to his people, to all the noblemen of his land. Also in the past many a wise man had bewailed the daring chief's venture. Those who expected redress for misfortunes from him had hoped that the royal prince might prosper and attain his father's rank, guard the people, the hoard, and the stronghold, realm of heroes and homeland of the Danes. Beowulf was beloved by his friends and all mankind, whereas crime took possession of Heremod.

Now the returning warriors raced their horses over the roads strewn with yellow sand. The morning light was hastening on. Many a valiant man went to the high wall to see the curious wonder; so too the king himself, guardian of the ring hoard, came from his wife's chambers. The glorious lord, famous for his nobility, came with a great company, and his queen also traversed the mead-path with a troop of women.

Hrothgar went to the hall; as he stood on the flight of steps

---

[11] A Danish king, presumably predecessor of Scyld Scefing; regarded as the prototype of the bad king.

and looked at the steep golden roof and Grendel's hand, he said: "For this sight, may thanks be offered to the Almighty at once! I have. endured many horrors and much grief at Grendel's hand. God, the King of Glory, can always work wonder after wonder! Not long ago I did not expect to see a remedy for any of my woes; the best of houses stood stained with blood, gory from battle—a great sorrow to all the wise counselors. They did not think they would ever be able to protect the stronghold of the people from foes, demons, and evil spirits. Now a warrior has done the deed—through God's might—that none of us were skillful enough to accomplish before. Indeed, if the woman who bore such a son into the world still lives, she may say that the Eternal Lord was gracious to her in her childbearing.

"Now, Beowulf, best of men, I will love you in my heart as my own son; keep this new kinship well from now on. You shall not lack any worldly goods that are within my power. I have often given a reward for less, and honored with treasure a lesser man, inferior in battle. You have done such deeds that your fame will live forever. May the Almighty reward you with good, as He did just now!"

Beowulf answered, "It was with good will that we did that deed of valor, undertook that fight, and boldly dared the strength of the mysterious enemy. I greatly wish that you could have seen him yourself—the fiend in all his trappings, weary to death. I intended to pin him down to his deathbed quickly with hard grasps, so that he should lie low, struggling for life because of my handgrip, unless his body should escape. I could not hinder his going, when the Lord did not wish it so; I could not hold the deadly foe firmly. The fiend was too powerful in his departure. Nevertheless he left his hand to save his life, his arm and shoulder remained behind; nor did the wretch gain any consolation. No longer shall the evildoer live, hardened in sins, for sorrow has seized him close in its forceful grip, its evil fetters. There the guilty creature must await the great judgment, and find how the glorious Lord will impose his sentence on him."

Unferth was a more silent man now; he made no boasting speeches about war deeds after the court had seen the hand hung under the high roof, the fiend's fingers put there because of the hero's prowess—the tips of those fingers, at the nails, were just like steel; the claws of the heathen fighter were hateful and monstrous. Everyone said that no hard weapon, not even the best of heirloom swords, could touch the bloody battle-hand of the monster in a way that could harm it.

At once orders were given to decorate Heorot. Many men and women there decked that wine building with their hands. Tapestries ornamented with gold shone on the walls, and there were many wonderful sights for everyone to gaze on. That splendid house, bound fast with iron bands within, was very much broken up, and the hinges were cracked apart; only the roof survived uninjured in every respect when the monster, stained with guilty deeds, turned in flight, despairing of life. It is not easy to flee death: let him try it who will, he must needs seek out the place prepared for the souls of men, for all who dwell on earth, when his body sleeps fast in the grave after the feast of life.

6. Hrothgar's Feast (lines 1008–1235)

Beowulf is rewarded with princely gifts and hears the minstrel tell the story of Finn and Hengest

Now the proper time came for Hrothgar to go to the hall; the king wished to partake of the feast himself. They say that never did a band of people bear themselves better, or gather in greater number, around their lord. The men turned to the benches and rejoiced in the feast; the mighty kinsmen Hrothgar and Hrothulf[12] duly received many a cup of mead in the high hall. Herorot was filled with friends; at that time the Danes had no thought of treachery.

As a reward of victory, Hrothgar gave Beowulf a golden banner, a decorated battle standard, a helmet and a coat of mail, and many men saw a glorious, precious sword brought before the war-

[12] Hrothgar's nephew (see genealogical tables). We know from other sources that Wealhtheow's confidence in him was misplaced: after the death of Hrothgar, he usurped the throne.

rior. Beowulf received the cup on the hall floor—he did not need to be ashamed of his rich gifts before the warriors! Few men have given four such golden treasures to others at the banquet in true friendship. Around the top of the helmet a rim wound with wires protected the head above, so that when the warrior went forth against his foes no hard sword could injure him severely in the battle.

Then the king ordered eight gold-bridled horses to be led onto the floor, into the enclosure; on one of them was a saddle skillfully decorated, ornamented with jewels. This was the war saddle of the king himself, which Hrothgar had used when he wanted to join in swordplay—and never did the valor of that famous chief fail; he was always at the front when the slaughtered fell. And then the ruler of the Danes gave all this into Beowulf's keeping, horses and weapons, and bade him enjoy them well. The glorious lord, guardian of the treasure of heroes, paid for the combat with horses and treasure in such a manly fashion that no man with a regard for the truth could find fault with him.

Beyond that he gave precious heirlooms over the mead-bench to each of the band of nobles who came with Beowulf on the ocean voyage, and he ordered gold to be given for the one whom Grendel had foully murdered before—as the monster would have done to more of them, if God in his wisdom had not put fate and the courage of man in his way. The Lord controlled all of mankind, as he still does now; therefore discernment, forethought of mind, is always best. He who lives long in the world here in these struggles shall experience many things, both good and bad!

Then there was song and music before the Danish king; the harp was touched, many a tale was told, and Hrothgar's minstrel recited a lay to entertain them along the mead-bench.

He told of the sons of Finn,[13] of how disaster befell them, and how Hnaef, the hero of the Danes, fell on the Frisian battlefield.

---

[13] King of the Frisians and Jutes. Apparently his marriage to the Danish princess Hildeburh was intended to settle a feud; it did not, for on a visit to Finn's court Hnaef, Hildeburh's brother, was killed. The Danes (under the leadership of Hengest) and Frisians fought on for several days, until an uneasy truce was arranged. The *Beowulf* poet tells us what happened after that.

Indeed, Hildeburh had little cause to praise the good faith of the Jutes. Through no fault of hers, she was deprived of her dear ones in the fray; son and brother fell doomed, wounded by the spear. That was a sad lady! It was not for nothing that she mourned the decree of fate when morning came and by daylight she could see her kinsmen murdered, where before she had enjoyed the greatest earthly pleasures.

War had taken away all of Finn's thanes, save only a few, so that he could not take the field at all to fight it out against Hengest; but they offered him terms. The Frisians yielded them room in another building, the hall and high seat, and they were to share equal power with the sons of the Jutes; at treasure giving, Finn should honor the Danes each day and present rings to Hengest's troops, giving them just as much golden treasure as he gave to cheer the Frisian race with in the beer hall. On both sides they agreed to a firm peace treaty.

Finn made solemn vows to Hengest: that he would hold the survivors in honor according to the judgment of wise counselors; and that no man there should break the agreement by word or deed, or ever complain of it in malice, although they would be following the slayer of their leader—they had to do this since they were without a lord. Then if any one of the Frisians were to recall the feud in provocative speech, the sword's edge should settle it.

The funeral pyre was prepared and gold was brought from the hoard. Hnaef, the best of the Danish warriors, was ready to be placed on the funeral pyre. At the pyre everyone could see bloodstained mail and the golden images of boars, iron-hard on the helmets, and many a nobleman killed with wounds—no few had fallen in the slaughter. Hildeburh then ordered her own son entrusted to the heat in Hnaef's pyre, his body to be burned and put on the pyre by his uncle's shoulder. The lady lamented and uttered mournful dirges. The warrior was raised up, and the greatest of funeral pyres wound to the clouds, roared before the mounds; heads melted, and open wounds burst—blood sprang out from the grievous bodily wounds. Flame, greediest of spirits, swallowed all those of both nations whom war had carried off; their glory had departed.

Deprived of their friends, the warriors departed to find their homes; they went to their dwellings and strongholds in Friesland. But Hengest, most miserable, still stayed on with Finn through that terrible winter. His thoughts turned to his home, although he could not sail a boat on the sea, for the ocean welled with storm, contending with the wind; winter locked the waves in its icy bond, until the new year came to the dwellings of men—as it still does now; the glorious bright weather holds to its proper time. Then winter was shaken off, the bosom of earth fair, and the exile was eager to leave the dwelling of his host.

But he wanted vengeance even more than the sea voyage. He wished to bring about an encounter where he might use his sword in memory of the fallen sons of the Jutes. Therefore he did not refuse to battle against Finn when Hunlafing put the Battleflame, best of swords, on his lap; that blade was well known among the Jutes.

Thus in his turn Finn also met with death by the sword in his own home, when Guthlaf and Oslaf had complained of the grim attack after the sea voyage, blamed it for many woes, and the restless spirit in the heart could forbear no longer. Then the hall was reddened with the life's blood of enemies; Finn, the king, was slain, and the queen taken. The Danish warriors took all the king's household property to the ships—all the precious jewels they could find in Finn's home. They brought the noble wife over the sea to the Danes, and led her to her people.

·   ·   ·

The lay was sung; the gleeman's tale was over. Mirth was renewed and the noise of men at the bench resounded as cupbearers poured wine from wonderful vessels. Then Wealhtheow, wearing a golden circlet, came forward to where the two leaders, Hrothgar and his nephew, sat; at that time there was still peace between them, each one was true to the other. (Unferth, the speaker, sat at the feet of the Danish lord; each of them trusted his spirit, and believed that he had great courage, although he may not have been honorable in swordplay with his kinsmen.) The Lady of the Danes then spoke: "Take this cup, my dear sovereign lord. Rejoice, generous friend of men, and speak to the Geats with words of friendship, as you should. Be gracious to the Geats, remembering how many gifts you have gathered from far and near.

"Someone has told me that you wish to have this hero as a son. Heorot is cleansed, the bright ring hall; make use of generous rewards while you can, but leave the people and kingdom to your kinfolk when the fated time comes for you to depart. I know my gracious Hrothulf; he will protect our children honorably, if you, my lord, should leave the world before he does. I am sure that if he remembers all the kindnesses we did for him as a child, to his pleasure and honor, he will treat our sons well in turn."

Then she turned to the bench where her sons, Hrethric and Hrothmund, were seated with other young warriors, sons of heroes; there Beowulf, the brave Geat, sat by the two brothers.

The cup was carried to him and cordially offered along with wrought gold, presented graciously: two arm ornaments, mail, rings, and the greatest collar ever heard of on earth; there could have been no better treasure in any hoard of heroes since Hama[14] carried away the necklace of the Brisings to the glorious stronghold—he took the precious gems in their fine settings and fled Ermanaric's crafty enmity, before he chose eternal gain. (Hygelac, king of the Geats, had that circlet with him on his last campaign, when he defended the treasure under his banner and guarded the spoil of battle. Fate took him off when in his pride he courted trouble and made war on the Frisians. When he bore the treasure with its precious stones over the waves, the powerful lord fell there beneath his shield. The king's body with his coat of mail and the circlet as well passed into the power of the Franks. Lesser warriors plundered the slain after the slaughter of the battle, when the corpses of the Geatish people covered the battlefield.)

The hall rang with applause. Wealhtheow said before the company, "Enjoy this circlet, beloved Beowulf, in all prosperity; make use of this precious mail, and prosper well; show your strength, and be a kind counselor to these boys. I will remember to reward you for it. You have brought it about that men will al-

---

[14] A legendary Germanic hero; the treasure he is said to have stolen from Ermanaric (the historical king of the East Goths) is probably a magic necklace made, according to some sources, for the goddess Freyja by the Brisings.

ways honor you, near and far—even as far as the sea, home of the winds, encircles the shores. Be blessed as long as you live, prince! I wish you all prosperity. Be a kind friend to my son, favored one! Here each nobleman is true to the other, kindly in spirit and loyal to his liege lord; the thanes are united, the people of good will; the retainers have their fill of wine and do as I bid."

Then she went to her seat. The choicest of banquets was before them, and the men enjoyed the wine. They did not know the doom, grim destiny, which many of the nobles would meet.

7. Grendel's Mother (lines 1235–1491)

A she-monster avenges the death of her son

When evening came, Hrothgar, the powerful king, repaired to his dwelling to take his rest, and a great number of earls occupied the building, as they had often done before. They cleared away the bench planks and spread out beds and cushions. At least one of the beer drinkers turned to his rest in the hall, doomed, ready to die. They placed their shining wooden shields at their heads, and on the bench over each warrior could be seen his towering war helmet and his mail and mighty spear; it was their custom to be always ready for war, whether at home or away, whenever their liege lord should have need of them—it was a good band.

They sank down to fall asleep. One paid dearly for that evening's rest, as had often been the case before when Grendel occupied the gold hall and committed evil, until the end came and he met death after all his crimes. Now it became clear and obvious to everyone that an avenger had survived the hateful monster, and still lived after the terrible struggle was over. Grendel's mother, a she-monster, brooded over her misery.

She was among those who had had to live in the dreadful cold water, ever since Cain murdered his own brother, his father's son, and went forth outlawed, branded a murderer, to flee the joys of men and inhabit the wastelands. He was the ancestor of many doomed spirits, of whom Grendel, the hateful, accursed oppressor, was one: he who found a wakeful man awaiting battle at Heorot. There the monster had laid hold of him, but he remembered his mighty strength, that liberal gift which God had given him, and trusted himself to the Almighty for grace, help, and support. Thus Beowulf had overcome the fiend and subdued the hellish spirit. Humiliated and cut off from joy, the enemy of mankind then departed to seek his deathbed. Still, his mother, gloomy and greedy, intended to go on a sorry journey to avenge the death of her son.

And so she came to Heorot, where the Danes slept about the hall: those noblemen there suffered a sudden reverse of fortune when Grendel's mother came in. Their terror was less by just as much as a woman's strength in war is less in comparison with that of armed men, when the trusty edge of the hammer-forged sword, stained with blood, cuts against the boar over the helmet. Then blades were drawn in the hall, swords brought down from over the seats, and many a shield was raised firmly in hand—but no one thought of helmet or coat of mail when the sudden horror seized him.

She had to hurry: she wanted to get out of there and save her life when she had been discovered. Quickly, she seized one of the warriors in a firm grasp, then went to the fen. The man she killed in his resting-place was a glorious hero and dearest to Hrothgar of all the counselors in the world. (Beowulf was not there: after the treasure giving, another lodging had been assigned to the glorious Geat.)

There was an outcry in Heorot. She took the familiar hand covered with blood. New sorrow had come again to the building; nor did anyone benefit from the exchange, for on both sides they had to pay with the lives of friends.

The wise old king, the gray-haired warrior, was sad at heart when he knew that his chief thane lay lifeless, that his dearest retainer was dead. Beowulf, the man blessed with victory, was quickly summoned to his chamber. At daybreak the noble champion went with his companions to where the venerable king was waiting and wondering whether the Almighty would ever work a change for him, as he pondered the sad tidings. The hero went across the floor with his troop—the wood of the hall resounded—

and addressed the Danish ruler, asking him whether the night had been as agreeable as he desired.

Hrothgar replied, "Do not ask about joys! Sorrow has come again to the Danish people. Aeschere is dead, Yrmenlaf's older brother, my confidant and counselor, my comrade when we defended our heads in battle where troops clashed and struck against the boar-helmets. A nobleman should be such as Aeschere was—an excellent prince! A wandering murderous demon has killed him in Heorot.

"I do not know where the horrible being went, glorying in carrion and glad of prey. She avenged the death of Grendel, whom you killed violently with your handgrasp last night, because he had too long diminished and destroyed my people. He fell in war, his life forfeit. And now another comes, a mighty, wicked ravager who wishes to avenge her kinsman—and has gone far indeed to even the feud, as it may seem to many a thane who mourns for his chieftain in spirit. It is a sore distress of heart, for now that generous hand which was always ready to help is stilled.

"I have heard my people, countrymen, and counselors say that they saw two such great wanderers, alien spirits, keeping the moor. One of them, as they could definitely see, was in the likeness of a woman; the other wretched creature trod the paths of exile in the form of a man—him the countrymen used to call Grendel. They know nothing of his father, nor whether other evil spirits preceded him. They inhabit uncharted country, the retreat of wolves: windy cliffs and dangerous fen paths, where a mountain stream goes down under the misty bluffs and the flood runs under the earth. It is not many miles from here that the mere stands. Over it hang frosty groves, the firmly rooted wood shadowing the water. Every night a fearful wonder can be seen there: fire on the water.

"There is no man alive who knows the bottom of that mere. Although the antlered hart, when pursued by hounds and driven far over the heath, may seek out the forest, still he will sooner give up his life on the bank than jump in to save his head. That is not a safe place. There surging water rises up dark towards the clouds when wind stirs up hateful storms, until the air becomes gloomy and the heavens weep. Now, again, you alone can help.

You do not know that region, the dangerous place where you might find the polluted creature: seek it if you dare! I will reward you for the fight with riches of twisted gold and ancient treasure, as I did before, if you get away."

Beowulf answered, "Do not sorrow, wise lord! It is better for a man to avenge his friend rather than to mourn greatly. Each of us must expect an end of this world's life. Let him who can acquire glory before death; that is best for a warrior in the end, when life is gone. Rise, protector of the kingdom: let us go quickly and look at the track of Grendel's kinswoman. I promise this to you: she shall not escape to cover, neither in the bosom of the earth nor in the mountain wood, nor on the bottom of the ocean —go where she will. Have patience this day with all your sorrows as I expect you to."

The old man then sprang up and thanked God, the mighty Lord, for the hero's words.

A horse with twisted mane was bridled for Hrothgar and the prince went forth in a stately manner. A band on foot advanced, bearing shields. They saw many tracks along the paths of the wood, along the ground where she had journeyed directly forward over the murky moor, bearing the lifeless body of the best thane of all those that ruled at home with Hrothgar. The king went over steep stone cliffs and along narrow paths where it was necessary to go one by one, along unknown ways, over steep bluffs and past many dens of water monsters; with a few experienced men he went on in front to examine the place, until he suddenly found mountain trees leaning over gray stones, a joyless wood. The water stood below, bloody and turbid. It was a painful thing for all the Danes to suffer, a great grief to every thane, when they encountered Aeschere's head on the waterside cliff.

The water boiled with blood, hot gore, as the people gazed at it. From time to time a horn sounded an eager battle song. The troop all sat down, and saw in the water many serpents, strange sea dragons exploring the brine, and water monsters lying on the slopes of the bluff, like those that many a morning take their ill-omened way on the high sea—such serpents and wild beasts. They rushed away in bitter fury when they heard the clear song of the war horn.

The chief of the Geats took his bow and ended the life of one of them; the hard war arrow struck in his vitals and finished his struggle with the waves. He was the slower at swimming in the mere as death took him off: soon he was hard pressed in the waves with barbed boar-spears; the wondrous wave-roamer was attacked with violence and drawn to the cliff. The men gazed at the terrible enemy.

Beowulf arrayed himself in noble armor—he did not worry about his life at all. His broad and well-woven coat of mail was to try out the waters—that garment which could protect his body so that the grip of battle could not injure his head, the malicious grasp of the angry foe could not harm his life. His head was protected by his shining helmet, which was to stir up the bottom of the mere, to seek the surging water; it was enriched with treasure and encircled with a splendid band as the smith had made it in far-off days, when he fashioned it wonderfully and adorned it with swine images so that afterwards no sword could bite through it.

And, in his need, Unferth, Hrothgar's speaker, loaned him a weapon that was not the least of helps: Hrunting was the name of the hilted sword. That was among the best of ancient treasures. The edge was iron, colored with poison-stripes, hardened with blood shed in battle—never had it failed any of the men who grasped it in their hands, this sword which dared to go on the perilous expedition to the hostile dwelling; it was not the first time that it was to perform valorous deeds. Indeed, as Unferth lent the weapon to the better swordsman, he gave no thought to what he had said before when he was drunk with wine; he himself did not dare to venture his life to accomplish deeds of valor under the waves. Thus he lost an opportunity to win glory and fame for courage. It was not so with the other, when he had arrayed himself for fighting.

Beowulf, son of Ecgtheow, spoke: "Wise and generous prince, glorious son of Healfdene, remember, now that I am ready for the venture, what we two said earlier: that if I should lose my life for your sake you would always stand in a father's place to me when I am gone. Be a protector to my retainers and companions if battle should take me. Also, beloved Hrothgar, send the treasures you gave to me on to Hygelac; then the lord of the Geats, the son of Hrethel, can see, when he looks at the golden treasure, that I found a lord of great munificence and enjoyed it while I could. And let Unferth have my ancient sword, the splendid heirloom with wavy ornament; he may have that hard blade. Either I will gain fame with Hrunting or death shall carry me off."

8. The Battle at the Bottom of the Mere
(lines 1492–1631)

Beowulf risks his life in the lair of the monsters

After these words, the leader of the Geats pressed on courageously—he did not wait for an answer. The surging water received the warrior. It was a good part of a day before he could see the bottom. Soon the grim and greedy monster, who had occupied the watery regions for a hundred half-years, found that a man was exploring the alien region from above. She grasped at him, and grabbed the hero in her horrible claws—but nevertheless she could not harm his body, which was unhurt because mail protected it all about; her hostile fingers could not penetrate the war shirt, the intertwined coat of mail.

When she reached the bottom, the she-wolf of the water bore the armed chieftain to her dwelling in such a way that, courageous as he was, he could not use his weapons. Many strange beings afflicted him in the water; many a sea beast tried to break his battle coat with its warlike tusks; many monsters pursued him. Then the hero saw that he was in some sort of enemy hall, where no water harmed him at all and its sudden rush could not touch him because of the roof of the chamber; he saw firelight, brilliant flames shining brightly.

Now the brave man could see the accursed monster, the mighty mere-woman. He did not hold back his blow, but gave a mighty rush with his sword so that the blade sang a fierce war song on her head. But the flashing sword would not bite or do her harm; the edge failed the prince in his need. It had endured many skirmishes before and had often sheared the helmet and mail of a doomed man: this was the first time that the glory of the precious treasure was diminished.

But the kinsman of Hygelac was resolute and intent on achieving brave deeds; his courage did not fail him at all. The angry warrior threw the ornamented sword so that the firm steel edge lay on the earth; he trusted in his own strength, his mighty handgrip. So must a man do when he hopes to gain long-lasting fame in war—he cannot worry about saving his life. The leader of the Geats did not flinch from the battle: he seized Grendel's mother by the shoulder. In a fury, the bold warrior flung the deadly foe so that she fell to the floor. She quickly retaliated with grim grasps and seized him; weary in spirit, the strongest of champions stumbled and fell down.

The demon pounced on the intruder, drew her knife, broad and bright of edge—she wished to avenge her child, her only son. The woven mail which covered Beowulf's shoulder protected his life and withstood the entry of point and edge. Ecgtheow's son, the Geatish champion, would have perished then under the earth if his armor, the hard war mail, had not given him help; and holy God brought about victory in battle. The wise Lord, Ruler of the heavens, easily decided the issue rightly, after Beowulf stood up again.

Among the armor in that place he saw a victorious sword: an ancient giant's sword, strong of edge, the glory of warriors. It was the choicest of weapons except that this good and splendid work of giants was too huge for any other man to carry in battle. The grim, fierce defender of the Danes seized the chained hilt and drew the ring-marked sword, despairing of life; angrily he struck so that it took her hard against the neck and broke the bone-rings. The sword cut right through her doomed body and she fell to the floor. The sword was bloody; the man rejoiced in his work.

The light gleamed; a glow shone forth within, just as the light of the skies shines brightly from heaven. Beowulf looked around the building and turned along the wall. He raised the weapon firmly by the hilt, angry and determined—that blade was not useless to the warrior, for he wished to repay Grendel at once for the many attacks which he had made on the Danes, many besides that one occasion when he killed Hrothgar's men in their sleep, when he ate fifteen sleeping men of the Danish tribe and carried off as many again, hideous booty! The fierce warrior had repaid him for that and now he found Grendel lying in his resting-place, wearied by war, dead of his injuries at the fight in Heorot. The corpse burst wide open when it suffered a blow after death; Beowulf cut off its head with a hard stroke of the sword.

Now the observant men who watched the mere with Hrothgar saw that the surging water was turbulent and stained with blood. The gray-haired veterans consulted together about the brave warrior, saying that they did not expect to see the noble man again; they did not think he would return in victory to their glorious prince. Many were agreed that the sea wolf must have destroyed him. Then came the ninth hour of the day.

The valiant Danes left the slope; Hrothgar went home from there. The foreigners sat sick at heart and stared at the mere; they wished to see their dear lord himself, but they did not expect it.

Meanwhile, after the battle, the sword began to shrink; the weapon looked like an icicle of battle. That was a great marvel: it melted just as ice does, when the Father releases the bond of frost; He who has power over times and seasons unbinds the fetters of the water—that is the True Lord. The chief of the Geats did not take any more of the valuable property in the cavern, although he saw many things there; he took only the head and ornamented hilt; the sword had already melted. The decorated blade had burnt up in the hot blood of the poisonous alien spirit who had died there. Soon the victor whose foes had fallen in battle was swimming again. He dove up through the water; the great expanse of the mere was completely cleansed when the monster had ended the days of its life and left this transitory world.

The seafarer came swimming to land. The stouthearted man rejoiced in the booty he brought from the sea, that great burden which he had with him. The group of mighty thanes went towards him and thanked God, rejoicing to see their lord safe and sound. The champion's helmet and coat of mail were quickly loosened from him. The lake grew torpid; the water, stained with the blood of battle, lay still under the clouds.

9. Heorot Cleansed (lines 1632–1812)

*Hrothgar congratulates Beowulf and speaks of
the duties of a ruler*

The valiant band set forth along the footpath, and went back re-
joicing on the familiar roads. The bold men bore the head from
the waterside cliff, but with great difficulty—it took the labors of
four men to bear Grendel's head to the hall on the shaft of a
spear.

Presently the fourteen Geats came to the hall; the courageous
leader crossed the cleared area around the mead-hall with the rest
of his troop and entered in. That daring man, honored for his
glorious deeds, went to greet Hrothgar. Grendel's head was carried
by the hair out upon the hall floor there where men drank before
the lords and their queen: the men gazed at the wondrous and
horrible sight.

Beowulf spoke: "Behold, son of Healfdene, lord of the Danes,
we have gladly brought these sea spoils which you see here to you
as a sign of success. I barely escaped with my life from the fight
under the water: the battle would have been lost at once if God
had not shielded me. I could not do anything in battle with
Hrunting, although it is a good weapon. But the Ruler of men,
Who has often guided those who are friendless, granted that I
might see a beautiful sword, a huge heirloom, hanging on the
wall; so I drew that weapon. Then, when I had an opportunity, I
killed the guardian of the house. But the blade, with its inter-
laced markings, burned up as the blood, the hottest of battle
gore, sprang out.

"I carried off the hilt from the enemies; I had avenged their
wicked deeds, the slaughter of Danes, as was fitting. Now I prom-
ise you that you can sleep in Heorot free from care among your
band of men, with all your thanes, the veterans and the youth;
and that you, lord of the Danes, need not dread injury to them,
death to your court, from that quarter, as you did before."

Then he gave the golden hilt, made by giants long ago, into

the hand of the gray-haired chief; that work of wonderful smiths came into the possession of the lord of the Danes after the downfall of the demons. That malicious creature, God's adversary, left this world, guilty of murder, and his mother with him; then the sword hilt came into the keeping of that best of earthly kings who gave out treasure in the Danish realm.

Hrothgar gazed at the hilt, the old heirloom on which was written the story of the beginning of ancient strife when the flood struck and the sea poured over the race of giants—they suffered terribly. That was a race estranged from the Eternal Lord, but in the end the Ruler punished them through the flood of the water. On the bright-gold sword guard it was also set down and marked correctly in runic letters from whom that sword was first made, that choicest of iron weapons with its twisted hilt and serpentine ornamentation.

Then the wise king spoke, and all were silent: "Indeed, the one who works right and truth among the people, the old guardian of the land who has a long memory, can say that this lord was of the noblest birth. My friend Beowulf, your glory is established far and wide, over all nations. You carry all your might steadily, with discretion of mind. I shall carry out the agreement we made before. You shall be a long-lasting comfort to your people, a help to warriors.

"Heremod was not so to the glorious Danes; he turned out to accomplish not their joy, but the slaughter and death of the Danish people. He killed his boon companions in his rages—his own close friends, until the ill-famed prince was exiled from human joys. Although mighty God raised him beyond all men in the enjoyment of power and might, nevertheless a bloodthirsty heart grew within his breast. He gave no rings to the Danes in order to win glory. He lived joyless, and suffered the result of strife, long, great affliction. Learn by this: understand manly generosity. I, being old in winters, tell this tale for your sake.

"It is wonderful to tell how mighty God, through His great magnanimous spirit, distributes wisdom, land, and noble rank to mankind; He has power over all. Sometimes He lets the spirit of a man of high descent meet every pleasure: gives him earthly joy in his homeland and a stronghold of men to hold: and renders regions of the world, a broad realm, so subject to him that in his folly he cannot imagine an end. His life is a perpetual feast; sickness and old age do not hinder him a bit, no trouble casts a shadow in his heart, nor does strife bring about fighting anywhere—the whole world bends to do his will. He knows nothing of a worse condition.

"But arrogance grows and flourishes within him; then the guardian, the keeper of the soul, sleeps. That sleep is too sound, and hedged about with troubles; the killer who shoots wickedly from his bow is very near. Then he cannot protect himself; he is struck in the breast with bitter arrows which no armor stops, the perverse and strange commands of the accursed spirit. That which he has held so long seems to him too little; he is niggardly and surly; he does not give out gold-plated rings honorably, and he forgets his latter end and does not think of the honors which God, the Lord of glory, gave him earlier. In the end it comes about that his mortal body withers and falls doomed; another succeeds him, one who gives out treasure without grieving—he does not guard the noble treasure anxiously!

"Keep yourself from such wickedness, dear Beowulf, best of men; choose what is better: eternal gains! Shun arrogance, famous champion. Now you are at the height of your power for a while, but before long it shall come to pass that illness or the sword will cut off your strength—or the fire will grip you, or flooding waters, or the attack with a knife, or the flight of spears, or dire old age; or perhaps the brightness of your eyes will lessen and become dim; presently death will overpower you, brave warrior.

"For a hundred seasons now I have governed the Danes and protected them in war from many nations around this earth, from ashen spears and sword blades, so that I did not count any under the compass of the skies as my adversary. But I suffered a reversal in my own home: sorrow succeeded joy when Grendel, enemy of men, invaded my hall; I suffered continual distress because of this persecution.

"Now may God, the eternal Lord, be thanked for this: that I have lived to gaze with my own eyes on that bloodstained head after the long strife! Now go to your seat and enjoy the pleasures of the banquet, victorious hero. We two shall share a great many treasures when morning comes."

The Geat was glad at heart and quickly went to seek out his seat, as the good king bade him. Then again, as before, a feast was handsomely set forth in the hall for the valiant warriors.

The cover of night grew deeper, dark over the troop of men. All the retainers arose, for the gray-haired prince of the Danes wished to go to his bed. The brave Geat warrior had great need of rest and, weary after his adventure, he was quickly led out by the chamberlains who attended courteously to all the needs which a seafaring nobleman would have had in those days.

Then the great-hearted man rested in the towering building, vaulted and decorated with gold; there the guest slept until the black raven blithely announced the coming of the sun. Then the light came quickly, brightness drove away the shadows. The warriors made haste, for they were eager to travel home to their people, and the hero wished to return to his distant ship.

Unferth ordered Hrunting brought and offered the sword to Beowulf, who thanked him for the gift, saying that he valued it as a good friend in battle, powerful in war; he did not find fault with the sword's edge. He was a man of noble spirit.

10. The Journey Back (lines 1813–1983)

Beowulf takes leave of Hrothgar and returns to the court of Hygelac

The warriors were ready in their armor, eager to depart. Now Beowulf went to the high seat where the king sat, and greeted Hrothgar. "We seafarers from far away wish to say that we are eager to return to Hygelac. We were well entertained here in every respect; you have treated us well. If I can do anything on earth, my lord, to earn more of your love with warlike deeds than I have yet done, I am ready at once. If I hear over the seas that neighbors threaten you with terror, as enemies did before, I will bring you a thousand thanes, heroes, to help you. Although Hygelac, lord of the Geats, is young, I know that he will help me with words and deeds, so that I may honor you well and bear a spear to help you when you have need of men. If, then, Hrethric, your son, should decide to go to the court of the Geats, he will find many friends there; other countries are best visited by a man who is himself powerful."

Hrothgar answered him, "The wise Lord sent these words into your mind. Never have I heard so young a man speak so wisely! You are strong in might and sage in mind, wise speaker. I expect that if it happens that the spear or grim warfare, disease or steel, should take Hygelac, your lord, while you are alive, the Geats have none better to choose as king and guardian of their treasure if you will rule the realm of your kin.

"Your spirit pleases me more the longer I know you, dear Beowulf. You have brought it about that there shall be peace between our peoples, the Geats and the Danes; there shall be no more of the strife and hostile acts which they endured before. As long as I govern this realm we shall exchange treasures; many men shall greet each other over the water with good things, the ring-prowed ship shall bring gifts and tokens of friendship over the sea. I know the people are steadfast in both enmity and friendship, blameless in every way, according to ancient custom."

Then the king gave Beowulf twelve more treasures, and bade him go safely to his people with the treasure and quickly return again. Then the most noble lord of the Danes kissed that best of thanes and clasped him by the neck; tears fell from the eyes of the gray-haired king. The wise old man knew there were two possibilities, but he thought one most likely: that they would not see each other again. The man was so dear to him that he could not hold back his emotion, for in his breast, firm in his heart, affection for the hero moved him.

Splendidly decked with gold, Beowulf left him, and went over the grassy earth, exulting in his treasure. The ship, riding at anchor, awaited its owner. As they went, Hrothgar's gift was praised; he was a king blameless in every way, until old age, which harms all too many, robbed him of his might.

The courageous troop of young men came to the water, wearing their coats of ring-mail. The coast guard saw the band returning, as before he had seen them arrive. He did not greet the visitors insultingly from the brow of the cliff, but rode towards them, saying that these warriors going to the ship in their bright armor would be indeed welcomed by the Geatish people. The vessel on the beach was laden with battle gear; the ring-prowed ship was filled with horses and treasures—the mast towered over Hrothgar's hoard of treasures. Beowulf gave the guard a sword wound with gold, so that afterwards he was the more honored on the mead-bench because of that heirloom treasure.

The ship went out, stirring up the deep water, and left the Danish land. A cloth sail was raised on the mast and made fast with rope. The wooden ship groaned. No wind over the waves drove her from her course and the vessel proceeded, floated foamy necked over the waves; the ship with its bound prow went forward over the ocean streams until they could see the Geatish cliffs, the familiar headlands.

Driven by the wind, the keel pressed on until it stood on the land. Quickly the harbor guard came to the shore—for a long time now he had eagerly looked out far from the beach for these beloved men. He moored the great ship to the beach, and made it fast with anchor ropes, so that the force of the waves could not drive the vessel away from them.

Beowulf ordered the noble treasure, precious things and plated gold, carried up. He had not far to go to find his lord, Hygelac, son of Hrethel, for he and his comrades dwelt near the sea wall. Hygelac's hall was splendid, the king valiant and noble, and the queen very young: Hygd was wise and accomplished, although she had not lived many winters within the hall-fort. She was not mean and niggardly with gifts of valuable treasure to the Geatish people.

She was not like the proud queen Thryth, who committed terrible crimes. No brave courtier dared be so bold as to stare openly at Thryth when he was not her husband; if he did, he knew that bonds of death were in store for him—soon after he was seized, a knife would be brought; the ornamented sword would settle the matter. Death would be the upshot. Such a custom is not fitting for a queen, even though she is beautiful; it is not queenly for a gentle lady to deprive a good man of his life because of pretended insult.

However, Hemming's kinsman, Offa,[15] stopped all that. Men
said over the ale-bench that she gave up her destructive ways after
she was given, decked with gold, to that most noble young cham-
pion; her hostile acts ceased after she had gone to Offa's hall, ac-
cording to her father's bidding, in a journey over the yellow-
green sea. There she made good use of her destined life on the
throne and as long as she lived she was famed for her goodness,
and held great love for that chief of heroes, who was, they say, the
best of all men on earth. Offa was widely exalted for his generosi-
ty and success in war; the bold man governed his native land
wisely. To him was born Eomor, help of heroes, kinsman of
Hemming, and grandson of Garmund; a warrior skillful in battle.

—Beowulf and his companions went off along the sand; they
trod along the sea strand, the wide shores, as the sun, light of the
world, came hastening from the south. They went on quickly to
the place where they understood that their good young warrior-
king, slayer of Ongentheow, dealt out rings within his strong-
hold. Hygelac was told at once of Beowulf's arrival; he learned
that the hero, his comrade in arms, came into the enclosure alive,
returning safely to the court from the battle. Quickly room in the
hall was yielded to the troop, according to the king's orders.

Beowulf, back from his perilous journey, sat down with his
kinsman, Hygelac, after his ruler had greeted him ceremoniously
with earnest words. Queen Hygd passed around the hall with
mead cups; she treated the people kindly and put the cup of
strong drink in the warrior's hands.

11. Beowulf's Account of His Adventures
(lines 1983–2199)

*The hero tells what he did and saw at the
Danish court, and what he expects will happen
to it in the future*

Hygelac, who burned with curiosity, began to question his com-
rade about the seafaring Geat's adventures: "What happened to

---

[15] A legendary prehistoric king of the continental Angles, ancestor of the
historical Offa, king of Mercia (d. 796).

you on your journey, dear Beowulf, when you suddenly determined to seek out strife far away over the salt water and join battle at Heorot? Have you in any way remedied princely Hrothgar's well-known trouble? I brooded over your venture in great distress and sorrow; I had no faith in my dear friend's undertaking, and for a long time I entreated you not to approach the murderous demon at all, but to let the Danes settle the fight with Grendel themselves. I give thanks to God that I may see you safe and sound."

Beowulf answered, "My encounter with Grendel is no secret, lord Hygelac; many men have heard what a fight between us two took place there where he had brought such sorrow and misery to so many of the valiant Danes. I avenged all that, so that none of Grendel's kin on earth—whichever of that hateful race, enveloped in crime, lives longest—need boast of that night's clash.

First, I went to the hall to greet Hrothgar. When the glorious son of Healfdene knew my intentions, he assigned me a seat beside his own son at once. The company was merry; never in the world have I seen a court enjoy themselves more over the mead. From time to time the splendid queen, the people's peacemaker, passed all around the hall urging the young men to drink, and gave rings to many a man before she took her seat.

"At times, Hrothgar's daughter came before the veterans and bore the ale cup to all the noblemen in succession—I heard the hall dwellers call her Freawaru as she gave the studded vessel to the heroes. Young and gold adorned, she is betrothed to Ingeld,[16] the gracious son of Froda. Hrothgar, the protector of the Danes, has agreed to this; he considers it a good plan to settle many quarrels and deadly feuds by means of the woman. But it is very seldom that the deadly spear rests for long after a king has fallen, however admirable the bride may be.

"For it may displease the prince of the Heathobards (and all that nation's thanes) when he goes into the hall with his wife and sees the Danish lords splendidly entertained; the noble child of

---

[16] King of the Heathobards, enemies of the Danes. His father, Froda, had been killed by the Danes. Beowulf's prophecy of the failure of Hrothgar's attempt to settle the feud by marrying his daughter to Ingeld is all too true: from other sources we gather that it was a raid of the Heathobards which caused the burning of Heorot.

the Danes would be attended by veterans on whom shine heir-
looms which once belonged to the Heathobards: the strong, ring-
decorated treasure that their ancestors once owned, until they led
their comrades to destruction in the shieldplay and forfeited
their very lives. —Then, over the beer, looking at the treasure, an
old warrior might speak, one who remembers everything about
how men fell by the spear; a man grim of spirit.

"In his bitterness, he begins to try the temper of a young war-
rior with his secret thoughts in order to arouse war, and he says
words like these: 'My friend, do you recognize the sword which
your father bore to battle when he wore his grim helmet for the
last time—the excellent blade he had there where the Danes slew
him? The bold Danish warriors held the battlefield when With-
ergyld lay dead, and our heroes had fallen. Now the son of one of
the killers goes about here on our hall floor exulting in that
prize; he boasts of the murder and bears the treasure which you,
by right, should possess.'

"Thus, he urges him and continually reminds him with bitter
words, until the time shall come when the woman's thane lies
covered with blood, slaughtered with a stroke of the sword, his
life forfeited because of his father's deeds; while the other escapes
from there alive, for he knows that land well. Then on both sides
the oaths of lords are broken and Ingeld seethes with deadly hate;
his love for his wife shall be cooled by the waves of sorrow.

"Because this is likely to happen, I do not consider the friend-
ship of the Heathobards firm or their alliance with the Danes se-
cure.

"Now I shall go on and tell you about Grendel, so that you,
lord, may know what came of the mighty combat. After the sun
set, the angry demon came; the terrible night prowler sought us
out where we, as yet unharmed, guarded the hall. His attack
there was fatal to Hondscio—a deadly encounter for the doomed
man. That champion was the first victim, and Grendel devoured
the famous thane—he swallowed all of the good man's body. Yet
the bloody-toothed slayer, his mind set on destruction, was none
the readier to leave the hall empty-handed.

Confident of his own strength, he decided to try me, and
grasped at me eagerly. His glove hung down, wide and strange,
fastened with wonderfully made clasps—it was all cunningly made

by the skill of a devil, from dragon skins. The fierce evildoer wanted to put me in there as one of many innocent victims. This could not be when I stood up in anger.

"It would take too long to tell how I repaid the enemy of men for each of his evil acts; but, my prince, my deeds there exalted the reputation of your people. He escaped and enjoyed the privilege of life for a little while; but his right hand stayed behind at Heorot, and he was driven away abject, to fall in misery to the bottom of a mere.

"The lord of the Danes rewarded me with gold and many treasures, when the next day came and we sat down to the banquet. There was singing and merriment. The venerable king of the Danes told of days gone by; at times a warrior played the harp delightfully, or told a tale, both true and sad; at times the great old warrior, stiffened by age, would begin to mourn his youth and strength in battle: his heart was stirred as the aged man remembered many things.

"And so we took our pleasure there all day long, until another night came to the world. Then Grendel's mother was quickly ready for revenge; she came mourning, for death—and the bitter hatred of the Geats—had taken away her son. The she-monster avenged her child and boldly killed a man. There Aeschere, a sage counselor, was deprived of life. But when morning came the Danish people could not burn the dead man in the fire nor put their dear friend on the funeral pyre; for she bore off the body under the mountain stream in her fiendish grasp. For Hrothgar, that was the bitterest of the many sorrows which had long afflicted him.

"Then the unhappy lord implored me by your life to undertake a heroic task in the tumultuous water, to risk my life and do glorious deeds; he promised me reward. Then, as is widely known, I found the grim and horrible guardian of the deep in the surging water. There we were in hand-to-hand combat for some time; the water boiled with blood, and with a mighty sword I cut off the head of Grendel's mother in her hall. I barely managed to escape with my life, but I was not yet doomed; and King Hrothgar gave me many treasures afterwards.

"The king thus followed courtly custom. I did not by any means lose the rewards which are the due of might; Healfdene's son gave me treasures of the choicest. These I will bring to you, my king, to offer with good will. All my joys still depend on you; I have few near relatives aside from you, my Hygelac."

Beowulf ordered the men to bring in a boar-banner, a towering war helmet, a bright coat of mail, and a splendid sword; then he made this speech: "When Hrothgar gave me this battle gear, the wise prince asked me particularly to tell you its history first. He said that King Heorogar,[17] lord of the Danes, had it for a long time; however, he would not give the armor to his son, bold Heoroweard, although he was a loyal son to him. Make good use of it!"

Following these arms came four bay horses, swift and exactly matched: Beowulf made Hygelac a gift of both horses and treasures. This is what kinsmen should do instead of weaving a net of malice for each other, preparing death for their close comrades with stealthy craft. Hygelac's nephew was most loyal to him, and each had the other's welfare at heart.

It is also said that Beowulf gave Hygd the neckpiece (that splendid great treasure which the noble queen, Wealhtheow, had given him), as well as three graceful horses, bearing bright saddles; Hygd's breast was well adorned after she received that gift.

Thus did Beowulf, so famous for battles and valiant deeds, act as a brave man ought; his behavior was worthy of praise. He never struck down hearth-companions when drunk for he did not have a savage spirit; but with the greatest of human skill the valiant warrior took care of the liberal gifts which God had given him. In the past he had long been despised: the Geats did not consider him worthy, nor would the lord of the Geats show him much favor at the mead-bench; they thought that he was slothful, a feeble prince.—But all the hero's troubles had come to an end.

The king now ordered Hrethel's golden legacy brought in; there was no better sword than this precious treasure. He laid it in Beowulf's lap, and gave him seven thousand hides of land, a hall, and a throne. Both of them held inherited land in that nation, an estate, and ancestral home, but the greater realm belonged to Hygelac since he was higher in rank.

[17] Elder brother of Hrothgar—see genealogical tables, page 117.

PART II—Beowulf and the Dragon

1. The Dragon's Hoard (lines 2200–2396)

Many years—and many battles—later, a venge-
ful dragon lays waste the land of the Geats

In later days it came to pass, in the clash of battle, that Hygelac lay dead and Heardred was cut down behind the shield-wall, when the warlike Swedes sought him out among his warriors and attacked him violently—then the broad realm passed into Beowulf's hands. He ruled it well for fifty winters. But when the king, a venerable guardian of his land, was old, a certain creature began a reign of terror in the dark nights: a dragon, who kept watch over a hoard of treasure in its upland lair. Below that steep stone barrow lay a secret path. A certain man found his way there and groped near the heathen hoard: in his hand he took a large and valuable cup. The dragon, tricked in his sleep by the craft of the thief, made no secret of his loss or of his anger: the people of the neighborhood soon found out that he was enraged.

The thief did not break into the dragon's hoard of his own accord; he who injured the dragon so sorely did it not of his own free will, but in sore distress. A slave of a certain man, he had fled from hateful blows and was in need of a refuge. The guilty man penetrated into the dragon's lair where he soon discovered that a fearful horror lay in wait for the stranger. Nevertheless, the wretched man took the treasure and escaped the wrath of the horrible monster.

There were many such ancient treasures in that earth mound, for in days of old a certain careful man had hidden the precious riches there, the immense legacy of a noble race. Death had carried off the rest in earlier times, and the veteran of that band who lived the longest, guarding the wealth and mourning his friends, expected that the same fate would come to him, and that he would have very little time to enjoy the long-accumulated wealth.

Nearby, on the plain near the waves of the water, was a barrow, newly built by the headlands and made difficult of access. There the guardian of the rings took a great quantity of noble golden treasure, well worthy of being hoarded, and said these words: "Earth, guard the wealth of princes, now that warriors cannot. Indeed, it was from you that men won it earlier; now death in battle, fearful slaughter, has taken them off, and all of my people have left this life—they have seen the last of the joys of the hall.

"I have no one who can bear a sword or polish a precious drinking cup; the host has gone to another place. The strong helmet adorned with gold must be deprived of its adornment, for those whose duty it was to polish the armor now sleep; likewise the mail, which once endured the bite of iron weapons over clashing shields in battle, now crumbles away as the warriors did; never again can it travel afar with the warriors, side by side with heroes. The harp is no longer joyous; there is no merry song; no good hawk swings through the hall, nor does the swift horse beat his feet in the courtyard. Baleful death has banished many of the race of men."

Thus the last survivor of them all mournfully bewailed his sorrows; cheerless, he kept on, day and night, until the tide of death touched his heart.

The old oppressor of the night found the hoard standing open: he who, burning, seeks out barrows, the bare, malicious dragon who flies by night, surrounded by fire; the country dwellers dread him greatly. He sought out the hoard in the earth, where, old in winters, he guarded the heathen gold—but he was not a bit better off for it.

For three hundred winters the despoiler of the people guarded that great treasure house in the earth, until a certain man infuriated him, when he took the dragon's golden cup to his master, asking his lord for a compact of peace. He explored the hoard and carried off the treasure; and when his lord looked at the ancient work of men for the first time, the wretched man's boon was granted. Then the serpent awoke, and the trouble began.

The bold beast quickly moved among the stones and found the footprints of his enemy, who had stepped forward, with stealthy craft, near the dragon's head—one who is not doomed can easily pass through woe and misery unharmed, if he has God's favor. The guardian of the hoard searched eagerly along the ground: he wanted to find the man who had robbed him in his sleep. Burning, angry, he cast about the cave again and again in all directions—while he could find no man in that wilderness, he was more and more in the mood for battle. Many times he turned back to the barrow and looked for the precious cup, but it did not take him long to realize that someone had tampered with the gold, his great treasure.

The dragon waited impatiently until evening came; the vindictive creature was enraged: he wanted to revenge the theft of the precious drinking vessel with flames. When day had gone—none too soon to suit the dragon—he had no desire to wait in his barrow, but went out surrounded by fire and armed with flames. It was a terrible beginning for the people of the land, just as the end was quick and terrible for their lord.

The invader began to spew forth flames, burning the bright dwellings. The gleam of fire shone forth in enmity to men; the hateful air-flyer would not spare anything alive. The serpent's devastation was seen everywhere; the cruel enemy's persecution was all too evident—all saw how the destroyer hated and humbled the Geatish people. Then he hastened back to his hoard, his secret hall, before daytime: he had overwhelmed the countrymen with flame, fire, and burning, and now he trusted in his barrow, its warlike defense and wall; but that hope failed him.

Beowulf knew the extent of the horror at once, for his own home, best of buildings, had been consumed by the fire—the high throne of the Geats was destroyed. That was a terrible grief to the good man, the greatest of sorrows. The wise king feared that he had bitterly angered God, the eternal Lord, by some infringement of ancient law, and his breast seethed within with dark thoughts, which was not customary with him.

The fiery dragon had destroyed the people's fastness with his flames, and laid waste the land near the sea. The war king, lord of the Geats, resolved to take revenge on him for this.

Then he ordered a splendid iron shield made for him; he well knew that a wooden shield could not help him against flame. The long-famed nobleman was about to reach the end of his brief, passing days, this world's life, and the serpent, although he had guarded the hoard-wealth long, was to go together with him. The prince scorned to seek out the wide-flyer with a troop of men, a large army; nor did he dread the battle for himself, or care a whit for the serpent's strength and courage in fighting, for he had dared great difficulty, and survived many a contest in the crash of battle since the time when he had victoriously cleansed Hrothgar's hall and crushed Grendel and his hateful kin in battle.

That was no minor battle, either, when Hygelac was slain: when Hrethel's son, the people's dear lord, was struck down by the sword and died in Friesland. Beowulf got away from there through his strength and skill at swimming; alone, he had thirty sets of armor on his arm when he went to the sea. Those Hetware who came against him bearing shields had no cause to gloat over the fight on foot: few escaped from the warrior to seek their homes again.

Then Beowulf swam back over an expanse of the sea to his people, a wretched solitary survivor. There Hygd offered him riches and the realm, rings and throne, for she was afraid that her child could not hold the ancestral seat against foreign armies, now that Hygelac was dead. But nevertheless the nobleman would not heed the pleas of the bereaved people; not for any consideration would he be Heardred's lord, or assume the royal power. But he supported Heardred among the people with friendly advice, with good will and honor, until he became older and ruled the Geats.

Banished men, the sons of Ohthere,[18] came to Heardred over the seas. They had rebelled against Onela, the Swedish king, that best of the sea kings who dispensed treasure in Sweden. That caused the end of Heardred's life; the son of Hygelac gained nothing but a mortal wound. When Heardred lay dead, Onela went back to his own country, and let Beowulf hold the throne and rule the Geats. He was a good king.

---

[18] A Swedish prince, brother of Onela (see genealogical tables), father of Eanmund and Eadgils. The events stemming from the revolt of the sons of Ohthere are of major importance in Part II, since the increasingly serious feud between the Swedes and the Geats threatens the extinction of the Geat nation when Beowulf is dead (see Introduction).

In later days Beowulf did not forget the duty of revenging the death of a prince. He befriended deserted Eadgils; and supported him beyond the wide sea with an army, with warriors and weapons; and Eadgils avenged the feud with devastating attacks: he deprived King Onela of life.

2. The Fight with the Dragon, I (lines 2397–2591)

Beowulf bids his men farewell and goes alone to fight the dragon

Thus Beowulf had survived every battle, each dangerous conflict, and courageous deed, until the dáy came when he was to fight with the serpent. Then the lord of the Geats, swelling with anger, went forth with eleven companions to look at the dragon; he had learned the cause of the feud which so afflicted his people, for the celebrated vessel came into his possession by the hand of the informer. He who had caused the trouble to begin with, a downcast captive, was the thirteenth man in the troop: he had to show them the place humbly. Against his will, he went to where, as he knew, the earth hall was. The underground barrow, full of ornaments and filigreed jewelry, stood near the rolling sea, the crashing waves. The frightful guardian, the vigilant fighter, had long held the golden treasure under the earth—it was not easy for any man to get it.

The bold king sat on the headland; there the lord of the Geats spoke to his retainers. His spirit was sad, restless, and ready to depart: near at hand was the fate which was about to approach the old man and seek the treasure of his soul, sunder life from body. The prince's spirit was not enclosed in flesh much longer after this.

Beowulf, Ecgtheow's son, spoke: "In youth I survived many battles and times of war; I remember it all. I was seven years old when King Hrethel, the generous friend of the people, received me from my father; the king kept and guarded me, gave me wealth and sustenance, and bore our kinship in mind. I, as a warrior in the stronghold, was never any less dear to him than any one of his sons, Herebeald, or Haethcyn, or my dear Hygelac.

"The deathbed of the eldest was unsuitably spread for him by a kinsman, for Haethcyn struck down his brother, his rightful lord, with an arrow from his horn bow. He missed his mark and hit his kinsman, and thus one brother killed the other with a bloody shaft. That was an inexpiable killing: so serious a sin the thought of it wearies the mind; nevertheless, Herebeald's death had to go unavenged.

"It is hard for an old man to endure it when his young son swings on the gallows; he utters the dirge, a sorry song, when his son hangs as food for ravens, and he, though old and wise, cannot give him any help. Every morning he remembers his son's passing; he does not wish to wait for another heir in the stronghold, when one has experienced the torment of death's distress. Sorrowful, he sees the deserted wine hall in his son's dwelling, a windswept resting-place bereft of joy. The riders sleep, the heroes are in their graves; nor is there the sound of the harp, or sport in the enclosures, as there once was. When he goes to bed, alone, he sings a sorrowful song for his son; it seems to him that the fields and dwellings are all too spacious.

"In like manner the protector of the Geats endured overwhelming sorrow in his heart for Herebeald; there was no way for him to settle the feud with the murderer, nor could he pursue Haethcyn and punish him, although he had small love for him. Then, overwhelmed by his grief, Hrethel gave up the joys of men and chose the light of God. He left his sons lands and towns, as a prosperous man does, when he departed from life.

"Then there was conflict and warfare between the Swedes and the Geats over the wide water—a bitter feud arose after Hrethel died. Ongentheow's sons were bold and warlike, and they had no wish for peace across the sea, but often carried on terrible attacks near Hreosnabeorh. My kinsmen, Haethcyn and Hygelac, avenged these wicked deeds, as is well known; but it was a hard bargain for one of them since he paid for it with his life. The battle was fatal to Haethcyn, lord of the Geats. Then in the morning, Hygelac saw his brother avenged with the sword by Eofor, who fought with Ongentheow: his war helmet split, the old man of the Swedes fell, pale from battle. Eofor's hand remembered feuds enough: he did not withhold the deadly blow.

"Hygelac gave me land and a splendid dwelling. I repaid him for the treasure he gave men with my bright sword in battle, as it was given me to do. He had no need to seek among the Gifthas or the Danes, or in Sweden, for a lesser warrior to buy with treasure; I would always be in the vanguard of his troop, alone at the front —and I shall do battle thus while this sword endures, the sword which has always served me well, since I killed Daeghrefn, the champion of the Hugas, in the presence of the hosts. He could bring no armor as spoils of battle to the Frisian king; for the brave man, the Hugas' standard-bearer, fell in battle. He was not killed by the sword, but my grip stopped the beating of his heart, and broke his body. Now my hand and my strong sword's edge shall fight for the hoard."

Beowulf spoke proud words for the last time: "I engaged in many battles in youth; now I, as an aged king, shall still seek battle and achieve fame, if the wicked ravager will come out of the earth hall to meet me." Then he addressed each of the brave warriors, his dear comrades, for the last time: "I would not use a sword or weapon against the serpent if I knew how else I might grapple proudly with the monster, as I did long ago with Grendel; but I expect hot battle flames, a blast of venomous breath. Therefore I have my shield and coat of mail.

"I will not flee from the barrow's guardian so much as a foot, but what happens to us two at the wall shall be as Fate, lord of every man, decides. I am resolved to do without help against the flying monster. Wait on the barrow protected by your mail, men in armor, to see which of us two may better endure wounds after the bloody conflict. It is not your undertaking, nor within any man's power, if not mine alone, to fight against the dragon and win renown. I shall win gold by my valor—or else baleful war shall carry off your lord!"

The famous warrior rose by his shield. In his helmet and coat of mail he went under the stone cliffs, trusting in his own single-handed strength: such is not a coward's way. Then the mighty veteran of many battles, who had often been in the thick of the fighting when troops clashed together, saw stone arches standing by the wall, and a stream flowing out there from the barrow. The stream rushed hot with deadly fire, and no one could endure the hollow passage near the hoard for any length of time without being burnt by the dragon's flames.

The stouthearted lord of the Geats called out furiously: his voice penetrated under the gray stone, roaring a clear battle cry. When the guardian of the hoard recognized the man's voice his hatred was aroused—and there was no more time to ask for peace. First the monster's breath came out of the stone, hot battle vapor; the earth resounded. Under the barrow the hero raised his shield against the dreadful stranger, as the coiled creature's heart was stirred to fight. The good king had drawn his sword, an ancient heirloom sharp of edge, and each of the pair of enemies was in horror of the other.

The lord stood stouthearted with his high shield; he waited in his armor while the serpent quickly coiled himself together: then, the fiery dragon started to glide in coils, hastening to his destiny. But his shield protected the lord's life and body for less time than he wished: there, for the first time, Fate did not give him triumph in battle. The lord of the Geats raised his hand up and struck the terrible, many-colored monster with his ancestral sword, but the blade failed: the bright steel bit against the bone less strongly than the king's need dictated. He was oppressed by trouble.

Then the dragon, infuriated by the stroke, cast deadly fire and the hostile flames sprang everywhere. The king of the Geats could not boast of a glorious victory, for his naked sword failed in battle, which no trusty blade should have done. It was no pleasant journey that Beowulf was to take, for he must leave this world for another against his will, as every man must come to the end of his transitory days.

3. The Fight with the Dragon, II (lines 2591–2820)

Wiglaf helps his lord kill the dragon; but Beowulf is mortally wounded

Soon the fighters met each other again. The dragon took heart; his breast swelled as he breathed again—and he who had ruled a nation before was in great distress, surrounded by fire. No band of noble comrades stood courageously about him: they had fled into the wood to protect their lives. But there was one among them who was deeply grieved. Ties of kinship can never be put aside by a right-thinking man.

This good warrior was a prince of the Swedes called Wiglaf, son of Weohstan. When he saw that his lord was suffering from the heat under his helmet, he remembered the kindnesses Beowulf had shown to him before—the wealthy dwelling place of the Waegmundings[19] and every share of the common estate, as his father had had—then he could not hold back. He seized his yellow linden shield and drew his ancient sword, which had once belonged to Eanmund, son of Ohthere.[20]

When Eanmund was a friendless exile, Weohstan killed him in a sword fight, and bore the shining helmet, ringed mail, and ancient giant's sword to Eanmund's kinsmen. Onela rewarded Weohstan with Eanmund's armor and war gear—he said nothing of a feud, although Weohstan had killed his brother Ohthere's son. Weohstan kept the precious trappings for many seasons until his son could accomplish noble deeds like his old father; then, among the Geats, he gave Wiglaf his countless battle garments before the old man departed from life and took his way.

This was the first time that the young champion was to fight beside his noble lord. His courage did not dissolve, nor did his father's legacy fail in war; the serpent found this out when they had met together.

Sad at heart, Wiglaf upbraided his companions: "I remember the time when, as we drank mead, we promised the lord who gave us treasure in the beer hall that we would repay him for that war gear, helmets, and hard swords, if such a need befell him. Then he chose us out of the host for this expedition of his own will: he considered us worthy of glory, and gave us these treasures, because he considered us good warriors, keen helmet-wearers—although our lord intended to carry out this valorous work alone, since he has done more glorious deeds and daring acts than anyone else.

[19] The family to which Beowulf and Wiglaf belonged.
[20] See n. 17, p. 66.

"Now the day has come when our leader needs the support of mighty warriors. Let us go to him and help our war chief, as long as the heat of the grim fire-terror shall last! God knows that for my part I would much rather the flame swallowed up my body together with my lord. It does not seem right to me that we should bear our shields back home unless we may first kill the foe, and defend the life of the lord of the Geats. I know well that this is not what he deserves for his former deeds: that he alone of the Geat veterans should suffer harm and sink in battle; let us use sword and helmet, mail and battle garb together."

Then he advanced through the deadly fumes, bearing a shield to help his lord and saying: "Dear Beowulf, hold! You said in your youthful days that you would never let your fame decline as long as you live; now, resolute prince, famous for your deeds, you must defend your life with all your might. I shall help you!"

Hearing this, the dragon came back furiously; the horrible, malicious foe, bright with streaming fire, returned once more to attack his enemies, the hated men. Waves of fire advanced toward them. The linden shield burnt to the boss, and the young warrior's mail could give him no help: but when his own was destroyed by flames the youth quickly went under his kinsman's shield. The warlike king was still intent on glory, and he struck with his sword, using such great strength that it drove into the dragon's head. But the force of the blow completely shattered Beowulf's sword, Naegling; the bright heirloom failed in battle. It was his misfortune that no sword could help him in battle, for his hand was too strong. They say that his stroke overtaxed every sword; no matter how hard a weapon he bore to battle, it did not help him at all.

Now the enemy of men made up his mind to fight for the third time; the terrible, fiery dragon rushed at the hero when it saw its chance. The red-hot ferocious beast encircled Beowulf's neck with its bitter tusks, bathing him in his life's blood; blood flowed in streams.

But then, in this moment of need, Wiglaf, the warrior at the king's side, showed his valor, the skill and boldness which was his nature. The brave man paid no attention to the dragon's head, although his hand burned as he helped his kinsman, and he struck the hostile creature lower down; the shining sword sank in so that the fire began to die down at once. Now the king himself collected his wits and drew the deadly knife, keen and battle sharp, which he wore on his armor; the lord of the Geats slashed through the serpent in the middle. They had felled the enemy—valor had driven out its life, and the two kindred noblemen had killed it. This is what a man should do in time of need! This was to be the king's last victory, the last of this world's work that he would do.

For the wound which the earth dragon had inflicted on him before began to burn and swell and he soon knew that deadly poison raged within his body. The thoughtful prince went to sit on a seat by the wall; he looked on that work of giants and saw how the ancient barrow had stone arches within it, fast on pillars. His good thane took water in his hands and washed the blood-stained lord; he cared for his friend and ruler, wearied with battle, and unfastened his helmet.

Suffering as he was with deadly wounds, Beowulf knew well that he had reached the end of his allotted days of earthly joy; all his time was gone, death immeasurably near. He said, "Now I would have wished to give my armor to my son, if I had been granted an heir of the body to succeed me. I ruled the people fifty winters, and there was no king in any of the neighboring countries who dared to approach me with warriors and threaten me with terror. In my home I awaited my fate, kept what was my own well, and did not seek treacherous quarrels, nor swear false oaths. Though I suffer with fatal wounds, I may take joy in all that, since the Ruler of men need not lay the murder of kinsmen to my charge when my life leaves my body.

"Now go quickly, dear Wiglaf, to look at the hoard under the gray stone, since the serpent lies dead; now he sleeps sorely wounded, bereft of treasure. Make haste, so that I may look at the ancient wealth, the golden treasure, and clearly see the curious bright gems; then I may with greater comfort because of the wealth of treasure give up my life and the country I have long ruled."

Wiglaf quickly obeyed the words of his wounded lord. In his ring-mail he went under the roof of the barrow. When the brave young retainer, exulting in victory, went by the seat there, he saw glittering gold and many precious jewels lying on the ground, wonders on the wall, and the den of the serpent, the old night-flyer; he saw cups, the vessels of men of old, standing without a polisher and deprived of ornaments. There was many an old and rusty helmet and many skillfully twisted arm-rings.—Treasure, gold in the ground, can easily overpower any man, hide it who will.—Likewise he saw a golden banner hanging high over the hoard, the greatest of wonders woven by skillful hands; from this a light arose, so that he could perceive the surface of the floor and look over the ornaments. There was nothing to be seen of the serpent, for the sword's edge had carried him off.

Thus the hoard of old giants' work in the barrow was plundered by a man; he loaded cups and dishes in his bosom at his own will and also took the standard, brightest of banners. The old lord's iron-edged sword had already killed the creature who had so long guarded the treasure, waging war in the middle of the night with fierce, terrible, burning flames for the sake of the hoard, until he was killed.

Moved by the hoard, the messenger was eager to hasten back, anxiously wondering whether he would find the lord of the Geats alive there where he had left him, deprived of strength. Returning with the treasure he found the glorious prince his lord, bleeding, his life at an end; he began to throw water on him again, until words began to escape him.

The suffering old king looked at the gold and said: "I give thanks to the Lord—to the King of Glory, the eternal Ruler—for all the treasures that I now gaze on; I give thanks that I could gain such for my people before my death-day. Now I have sold my old lifespan for the hoard of treasure; now you must take care of the people's needs. I cannot be here longer. After I have been burned on the fire, have the warriors raise a splendid mound at the promontory of the sea; it shall be a remembrance to my people towering high on Hronesness, so that afterwards the seafarers who drive ships far over the dusky sea will call it Beowulf's barrow."

The bold lord undid the golden collar from his neck and gave it to the young warrior, along with his golden helmet, ring, and coat of mail, and bade him to use them well: "You are the last of our kin, the Waegmundings; fate has swept away all my kinsmen, the valorous noblemen, to their destiny. I shall follow them."

These were the last words the old man spoke before he was ready for the hot, hostile flames of his funeral pyre. His soul departed to seek the lot of the righteous.

4. Aftermath (lines 2821–3027)

The Geats foresee a time of trouble after the death of their king

It was a sad moment for the younger man when he saw his dear lord lying wretched on the ground, his life at an end. His slayer also lay dead; the terrible dragon had been overcome and destroyed. No longer could the coiled serpent keep watch over the treasure hoard, for the hammer-sharpened war sword had carried it off and the winged beast fell on the ground near the treasure house, stilled by its wounds. Never again did it fly through the air and appear in the middle of the night, proud of its precious property: it fell to the earth, killed by the hand of the warrior. Indeed, they say that no man of might, no matter how daring, could successfully rush against the breath of the venomous foe, or disturb the hoard of rings with his hands, if he found the watchful guardian in the barrow. Beowulf paid for that princely treasure with death; he and the dragon had both come to the end of their mortal life.

It was not long after this that the cowards came out of the wood: ten craven traitors together, who had not dared to use their javelins in their lord's great need. Shamefaced, they came with their shields and battle garments to the place where the old man lay and gazed at Wiglaf, who was sitting wearily near the shoulder of his lord, trying to rouse his king with water. But he did not succeed at all. No matter how much he wished it, he could not keep the chieftain alive on earth, nor turn aside the Ruler's decree; God's judgment ruled over every man, as it still does now.

Now those whose courage had failed did not have to wait long for a grim rebuke from the young champion. Wiglaf, Weohstan's son, looked at them with distaste; sick at heart, he said, "So: a man who wants to tell the truth can say that the king who gave you the treasures and warlike equipment that you stand in there —when over the ale-bench that lord gave the most splendid helmets and coats of mail that he could find, far and near, to his retainers in the hall—he completely threw away the war gear—to his sorrow. When war came upon him, the king had no need to boast of his comrades in battle. Nevertheless, God, the Ruler of victories, allowed him to avenge himself single-handed with his sword when he had need of courage. I could not give him much protection in battle, but I gave my kinsman what little help I could. The deadly foe weakened when I struck it with my sword: fire streamed less swiftly from its head.

"Too few defenders thronged around the prince when distress came upon him. Now the receiving of treasure and giving of swords, all the enjoyment of hereditary estate and comfort, shall cease for you and your kin; every man of your clan will have to turn away, deprived of the landowner's privileges, when noblemen far and wide hear of your flight, your shameful act. Death is better to every noble warrior than life in disgrace!"

Then he ordered the events of the battle to be announced in the stronghold up over the sea cliff, where the noblemen of the court had been sitting mournfully all through the morning; the warriors did not know whether to expect the death or the return of their dear lord. The messenger who rode along the the headland did not keep back the tiding, but said truthfully in the hearing of all, "Now the dear king of our people is fast on his deathbed; the lord of the Geats lies slaughtered by the dragon. His deadly enemy lies beside him, killed by knife wounds: he could not wound the monster with a sword at all. Wiglaf, son of Weohstan, sits by Beowulf, watching over his dead kinsman. Grieving, the nobleman holds his vigil over both friend and foe.

"Now the people must expect a time of strife, once the fall of the king becomes widely known among the Franks and the Frisians. Hard fighting was launched against the Hugas when Hygelac went with a sea army into the Frisian land, where the Hetwares assailed him in battles. With courage and superior strength, they brought about the fall of that mailed warrior; Hygelac fell among his troops. No more did the chieftain give prizes to his veterans. Since then the king of the Frisians has felt no kindness to us.

"Nor do I expect any peace or faith at all from the Swedish people, for it is widely known that Ongentheow[21] killed Haethcyn, son of Hrethel, near Ravenswood, where the Geatish people first arrogantly attacked the Swedes. Ohthere's father, old and terrible, soon repaid Haethcyn for his attack: he cut down that sea leader and rescued his own wife, the aged mother of Onela and Ohthere, bereft of her gold ornaments; and then he so pursued his deadly foes that they barely escaped, lordless, into Ravenswood. There with a large army he besieged the survivors, who were weary with wounds. All night long he threatened the unhappy band with destruction and said he would kill them with the sword in the morning, and put some on the gallows tree as a sport for the birds. With daybreak help came to the wretched men when they heard the sound of Hygelac's horn and trumpet, as the good man came after them with a host of tried warriors.

"The bloody trail of Swedes and Geats, how the people fought together in a gory conflict, was widely evident. Then the aged chieftain, sad at heart, went with his kinsmen to seek his fastness: King Ongentheow withdrew, for he had heard of Hygelac's fighting skill and he did not expect that he could resist the proud warrior's craft and fight against the seamen to defend his treasure, and the women and children, against the raiders. So he turned away again; the old man went behind an earth-wall. The Swedish people were given pursuit; Hygelac's banners went forth over the field of refuge until the Geats thronged about the enclosure.

"There gray-haired Ongentheow was brought to bay at sword's point, and the king was at Eofor's[22] mercy. Angrily, Wulf, son of Wonred, struck at Ongentheow with his weapon—because of that stroke his blood sprang forth under his hair in streams. But the old king of the Swedes was not afraid; he quickly turned and

---

[21] A Swedish king, father of Ohthere and Onela.
[22] A Geat warrior; brother of Wulf, son of Wonred; cf. p. 72.

paid back the deadly blow with a worse one. Now Wulf could not give a return blow to the old warrior, for Ongentheow cut through the helmet on his head first, so that he sank down stained with blood. He fell on the ground, but he was not yet doomed; he recovered, although the wound hurt him. When his brother lay wounded, Hygelac's thane, Eofor, with his broad sword broke through the protecting shield-wall to the giant helmet. Then the king fell: Ongentheow was mortally wounded. Many men bound up the wounds of Eofor's kinsman and quickly raised him up, now that it was their fortune to rule the battlefield. Meanwhile Eofor rifled Ongentheow and took his iron mail, and his strong hilted sword and helmet too; he bore the gray-haired king's armor to Hygelac, who received the ornaments and made him an honorable promise of rewards among the people—and he fulfilled it honorably.

"When Hygelac, lord of the Geats, had returned home, he repaid Eofor and Wulf for the battle with vast treasure: he gave each of them a hundred thousand units of land and linked rings. No man on earth had cause to blame him for the reward, since they had earned the reward for brave deeds. And then Hygelac gave Eofor his only daughter in marriage to grace his home, as a pledge of favor.

"That is the feud and enmity, mortal hatred between men, for which I expect that the people of the Swedes will attack us when they hear of the death of our lord, who previously guarded our treasure and kingdom against enemies; after the fall of other bold heroes, he helped the people and performed noble deeds.

"Now it would be best if we hastened to look at the king there, and bring to the funeral pyre him who gave us treasure. Nor shall only a part of the treasure hoard melt with the brave hero; that vast amount of gold, so grimly purchased, rings bought in the end with his own life: these the fire shall eat, the flames enfold. No nobleman shall wear an ornament as a remembrance, nor shall a lovely maiden have a necklace around her throat—sad of heart and bereft of gold, they shall tread a foreign country, not once, but many times, now that the leader of the army has laid aside laughter, joy, and mirth. Therefore many a morning-cold spear shall be gripped and lifted in men's hands; no more shall the sound of the harp wake the warriors; but the dark raven, eager for the doomed, shall have much to say and tell the eagle how he fared at the meal when he rifled the dead with the wolf."

5. Beowulf's Funeral (lines 3028–3182)

The hero's ashes are buried with the accursed gold

Thus the warrior told the unwelcome message; he did not lie as to events or words. The band rose up; all unhappy, with tears flowing, they went under Earnaness to see the wondrous sight. There they found him who gave them rings in former times lying on the sand, on his bed of rest; there the hero's last day had passed, the day in which the warlike king of the Geats died a wondrous death.

First they saw a stranger being there—the hateful serpent, lying opposite on the field; the fiery dragon, terrible in its coloring, was scorched with flames. It was fifty feet long in the place where it lay. Before, it had kept to the joyous air at night, then swooped downward to seek out its den; now it was still in death. It had made its last use of barrows. By the dragon stood cups and pitchers; dishes and precious swords lay there, rusty and eaten through, since they had lain there within the bosom of the earth a thousand winters.

Moreover, that huge heritage, the gold of men of old, had been bound with a spell so that no man could touch the ring hall—unless God himself, true King of victories (He is man's protection) granted to whom He would to open the hoard: even to whichever man seemed meet to Him.

It was clear now that the creature who had wrongly kept guard over the treasure in the wall had not prospered in his course. That guardian first killed a man with few peers, but that attack was severely avenged. No one knows where a famous hero may reach the end of his life, or when a man may no longer dwell with his kinsmen in the mead-hall. Thus it was for Beowulf when he sought battle with the barrow's guardian; he himself did not know what would bring about his parting from the world. For the glorious chieftains who put the treasure there laid a solemn curse on it until Doomsday, so that the man who plundered the place would be guilty of sin and confined to places of heathen damnation, held fast by hell-bonds and grievously tormented. Yet Beowulf had by no means gazed too eagerly on the owner's inheritance, abounding in gold.

Wiglaf, son of Weohstan, spoke: "For the one nobleman's sake, many others must often endure misery, as has happened to us. We could not advise the dear lord or counsel the king not to approach the dragon, but to let it lie where it had long been and inhabit its dwelling until the end of the world; he held to his high destiny. The hoard, grimly obtained, is opened to view; that fate which impelled the king here was too strong.

"I entered the barrow, and looked all around it, saw the precious objects of the building, when my way was clear: I had no friendly welcome to come in under the earth-wall. Hastily I seized a great burden of hoarded treasures in my hands and bore it back to my king.

"He was still alive, sound in mind and conscious. The old man said much in his suffering; he bade me greet you, and tell you to make a high barrow on the site of his funeral pyre: a great and glorious monument your lord deserved for his deeds, for when he was alive he was the most worthy warrior anywhere on earth. Now let us hurry and see the heap of curious gems again, the wonder under the wall; I will show you the way, so that you will see the rings and broad gold closely enough. Let the bier be prepared and quickly made ready when we come out; and there we shall carry our lord, the beloved man, to the place where he shall long abide in the keeping of the Almighty."

Then Wiglaf, Weohstan's brave son, gave orders that many houseowners be told to bring firewood from afar for the good lord: "Now the flame shall grow murky and the fire consume the ruler of warriors, who so often withstood the shower of iron when the storm of arrows, driven by the bowstrings, shook over the shield-wall, and the feathered shaft did its duty and sped the barb."

Next Wiglaf summoned together seven of the best of the king's band of retainers, and went under the enemy's roof with seven warriors; one who went at the head bore a torch in his hand. It was not decided by lot who plundered that hoard: when the men saw any part remain in the room without a guardian, lying forsaken, little did any hesitate to carry out the precious treasures hastily. They shoved the dragon over the cliff and let the waves take the guardian of the treasure, the flood embrace it. Then a vast amount of twisted gold of every kind was loaded on the wagon, and the noble gray-haired warrior was borne to Hronesness.

The people of the Geats prepared him a magnificent pyre on the ground, hung about with helmets, battle shields, and bright coats of mail, as he had requested. Then the lamenting warriors laid their glorious leader in the midst, and began to wake the greatest of funeral fires on the barrow. Wood smoke climbed up, dark over the flames; roaring fire mingled with weeping—the tumult of the wind subsided—until the fire had crumbled the body, hot to the heart. Sadly they complained of their distress, mourning the death of the their ruler; and a Geatish woman, with hair bound up, sorrowfully sang a sad lament for Beowulf, saying that she dreaded evil days of mourning, filled with great slaughter, terror of the enemy, harm and captivity. Heaven swallowed the smoke.

Then the Geatish people made a shelter on the promontory. It was high and broad, widely visible to seafarers; in ten days they finished building the famous warrior's beacon. Around the leavings of the fire they made the best wall skilled men could devise. In the barrow they put rings and jewels and all such adornments that warlike men had taken from the hoard; they left the noble treasure for the earth to hold, buried the gold in the soil, where it still lies now, as useless to men as before.

Twelve brave warriors, sons of princes, rode around the fire to express their sorrow and to lament the king. They composed an elegy about the hero, praising his nobility and extolling his deeds of valor, for it is meet that a man should praise his lord in words and love him in his heart, when his spirit leaves his body.

Thus the people of the Geats mourned their lord. They said that among the world's kings, he was the mildest and gentlest of men, most kind to his people and most eager for fame.

⊸≼ THE BATTLE OF
BRUNANBURH ≽⊶

In this year[1] King Athelstan, lord among earls, and Prince Edmund, his brother, won eternal glory with their swords in battle around Brunanburh. The sons of Edward cleft the enemy shield-wall, hewing through the shields with their well-forged blades—such was their nature: it was their heritage always to defend their land, its treasure and its homes, against all enemies in battle. The enemy perished; both Scots and vikings fell doomed. The field was flooded with the blood of men from the time in the morning when the sun, bright candle of the eternal Lord, swept up over the ground, until that glorious star, God's noble creation, sank to its rest.

There lay many warriors destroyed by spears—Norsemen, shot down over their shields, and Scots, spent, sated with war. All the day long the West Saxons pursued troops of foes, sternly cutting down the fleeing warriors from behind. Nor did the Mercians withhold hard combat from any of Olaf's companions, those who crossed the sea and sought out the land, fated to die in battle.

[1] 937; the poem, recording an historic battle, appears in the Anglo-Saxon Chronicle for this year. Athelstan (grandson of Alfred), king of the West Saxons, and his brother led the English to an important victory over an invading army of Norse vikings (led by Olaf) and Scots (led by King Constantine). The exact location of Brunanburh is not known, however.

Five young kings were left on the battlefield, laid to rest by the sword, as were seven of Olaf's earls, and a countless number of the army of vikings and Scots.

There the chief of the Norsemen was put to flight; need drove him to board his ship—with few followers—and push out to sea. The king sailed away over the dark waters, and thus escaped with his life. So also did the old campaigner flee to his home in the north: gray-haired Constantine had no cause to rejoice over the outcome of the battle. He was bereft of his kinsmen, deprived of friends slain on the battlefield, and had to abandon his son in the place of slaughter, where the young man was destroyed by wounds in the battle. The malicious old warrior did not need to boast—and no more did Olaf: with only a remnant of their army left, they had no occasion to exult that they had had the better in the deeds of war on the battlefield, when banners clashed, and spears and men encountered each other, when blows were traded on the field of slaughter as they fought against Edward's sons.

The Norsemen fled in their nailed ships, a dejected few who had escaped the spears. They sailed over the deep water to Dublin, returning to Ireland downcast and ashamed. Like them, the brothers, the king and the prince, went home together, returning to the land of the West Saxons exulting in victory. They let the dark-coated scavengers—the black raven with its horny beak, and the dusky-coated eagle, white in back—dispose of the corpses they left behind; the greedy war hawk and the gray wolf of the forest were left to enjoy the carrion.

Never before have so many people been killed in battle on this island, as the books of the wise men of old tell us, since the Angles and Saxons landed here, when the keen warriors came to Britain over the broad sea from the east, overcame the Welshmen, and won the land.

―ᗍ THE BATTLE OF
MALDON ᗏ―

... Then he[1] ordered one of the young men to dismount and drive
off his horse, for it was time to advance boldly, intent on deeds of
arms. The youth, a kinsman of Offa, seeing that the earl did not
intend to tolerate slackness, let his beloved hawk fly off from his
hands toward the wood, and went forward to fight. It was clear
that he did not wish to prove soft in battle when he took up his
weapons.

Eadric also wanted to help his lord in the fight, and took up
his spear; he had an undaunted spirit as long as he could bear
shield and broadsword, and he fulfilled his vow to fight before his
lord.

Now Byrhtnoth began to put his troops in order. He rode from
group to group, instructing them on how they should stand and
hold their position, bidding them hold their shields correctly and
firmly in their hands, and not to be at all afraid. When he had
ordered the army well, he alighted among the group where he
most wished to be, among his most devoted household retainers.

Then a messenger of the vikings came to the shore and sternly
called out, delivering a threatening message from the seafarers as
he stood on the bank: "Bold seamen send me to you. They bade me
tell you that you must send treasure quickly in exchange for pro-

---

[1] "He" is Byrhtnoth, leader of the English army. Unfortunately, *The Battle
of Maldon* is a fragment: both the beginning and the end have been lost.

tection, for it will be better for you to buy off this spear contest with tribute rather than to join hard battle with us. We need not slaughter each other if you have enough wealth: in exchange for your gold, we will make a firm truce. If you, who are the most powerful here, decide that you want to ransom your people, give the seamen the price they demand for peace, and we shall be glad to take the tribute money to our ships and put off to sea, holding peace with you."

Byrhtnoth raised his shield, waving his slender spear; angry and resolute, he answered: "Do you hear, seafarer, what this host says? This is what they will give you for tribute: spears with deadly points, heirloom swords, battle equipment that will not be of use to you in the fight. Viking messenger, go back and give your people news of hatred and defiance—for here with his troop stands a dauntless earl who intends to defend this country, Ethelred's realm, the people and land of my lord. The heathen shall fall in battle. I should think it a shame to let you take our tribute money back to your ship without a fight, now that you have come this far here into our land. You shall not get treasure so easily: before we give tribute, spear point and sword edge shall decide the terms for us in grim war."

Then he ordered men to take their shields and stand together on the river bank. Neither army could get at the other because of the water, for a flood tide came flowing after the ebb, and the seastreams joined. They stood on the shores of Pante's stream[2] in proud array, both the West Saxon troop and the viking army, nor could any of them harm each other, unless someone were killed by a flying arrow.

The tide went out. The sailors stood ready, many vikings, eager for war. Then Byrhtnoth, leader of warriors, ordered Wulfstan, a war-hardened veteran, to hold the causeway. Valiant, as was all his kindred (he was the son of Ceola), he struck down the first man bold enough to attempt the crossing. With Wulfstan stood other unafraid warriors, Alfhere and Maccus, two brave men who did not intend to take to flight there, but staunchly defended themselves against the enemies as long as they could bear weapons.

---

[2] The River Blackwater, in Essex.

When the invaders saw that the crossing was held against them by fierce guards, they turned to guile, and asked leave to come over the ford and lead their troops to the shore. And, in his pride, the leader undertook to yield too much land to the foe—Byrhthelm's son[3] called to them over the cold water, and the warriors listened: "A way is now opened for you; come to us quickly, to battle. God alone knows who shall be master of this battlefield."

The deadly sea wolves advanced. The vikings, untroubled by the water, bore their shields west over the shining stream of the Pante, to the land where Byrhtnoth and his warriors stood ready against the foes. There he ordered his men to form a shield-wall and stand firm against their enemies. Now fighting was near, and glory in battle; the time was come when doomed men should fall there. The battle cry was raised. Ravens circled, and eagles, eager for carrion, as a cry went up from the ground.

Hard spears, grimly sharp, flew from the warriors' hands; bows were busy, and points dug into shields. Bitter was the rush of battle. Men fell on both sides—young warriors lay dead. Wulfmar was wounded, Byrhtnoth's kinsman; he chose a resting-place among the slain—son of the leader's sister, he was quickly cut down by the sword. But the vikings were repaid: I heard that Edward killed one fiercely with his sword, not withholding his strokes, so that the doomed warrior fell at his feet. His lord thanked the chamberlain for that when he had the chance.

Thus the bold young men stood firm in battle, thinking only of who might be first in taking the lives of doomed warriors with their pointed weapons. Slaughtered men fell to the ground, but they stood steadfast under Byrhtnoth's ordering—he urged the young men to be intent on fighting if they wished to win fame at the Danes' expense. Strong in battle, he raised shield and weapons and advanced against the enemy, joining battle with one of the vikings.

In the end, the seaman wounded the lord with a spear of southern make. Byrhtnoth shoved against the spear with his shield edge, so that the shaft was shattered and the spearhead sprang out; then, enraged, he thrust at the proud viking who had given him the wound. The expert English warrior let his spear,

[3] I.e., Byrhtnoth.

guided by his hand, go through the young man's neck so that he pierced the raider fatally. Then he quickly stabbed another so that that one's mail burst apart and he was wounded in his breast through the linked rings of chain: a deadly point struck to his heart. The earl was the happier. The brave man laughed and said thanks to God for the day's work which had been granted to him.

But then one of the viking warriors let a spear fly from his hands in such a way that it went too far through Ethelred's noble thane. By his side stood a youth, not yet fully grown, who valiantly drew out the bloody spear from the warrior's side—he was Wulfstan's son, young Wulfmar; he sent the hard spear back again, killing the man who had so gravely wounded Wulfmar's lord. Now another armed man attacked the earl, wishing to carry off his treasure—armor, rings, and ornamented sword; Byrhtnoth drew his broad and gleaming blade from its sheath and struck at his attacker's corselet. Too quickly one of the seafarers hindered him, hacking at his arm, so that the golden-hilted sword fell to the ground. Never again could he hold his hard sword in his hand. Still the old veteran spoke to his men, encouraging the young warriors and urging his retainers forward.

But he could not stand firmly on his feet for long now. He looked to Heaven: "I thank Thee, Ruler of nations, for all the joys that I have experienced in this world. Now, merciful Lord, I have great need that Thou grant grace to my spirit, so that my soul may journey to Thee, and peacefully come into Thy power, Lord of angels. I beseech Thee that hell-fiends may not harm it."

Then heathen warriors cut him down, and both the men who stood by him, Alfnoth and Wulfmar, gave their lives beside their lord: both lay dead.

Those who did not want to be there now left the battle. Odda's son Godric was first in flight from the war, abandoning the good man who had often given him many a horse. He mounted his lord's own war horse, leaping into the trappings where he had no right to be, and his two brothers, Godwin and Godwig, galloped off with him; they did not care to fight, and turned away from the war, seeking safety in the wood. They fled into the wood to save their lives, and so did many more men than would have been at all fitting if they had remembered all that their lord had done for their benefit. Offa had once predicted this in council, saying that many who spoke boldly enough there would not want to hold out later in time of need.

The people's leader, Ethelred's earl, had fallen; all his close companions now saw that their lord lay dead. Undaunted, bold warriors went on in all haste, bent on one of two things: either to die or to avenge their beloved leader. Alfric's son encouraged them forward—the young warrior, Alfwin, spoke valiantly: "Remember the boasts we often made over the mead, when we warriors in the hall vowed there on the bench to follow our lord in hard combat; now it can be seen who is really brave. I want to make my noble descent clear, so that all may know that I came of a great Mercian family, and am the grandson of Ealhelm, a wise chieftain blessed with worldly goods. That people shall never have cause to reproach me that I wanted to desert this army and seek my home, now that my leader lies cut down in battle. That is the greatest of sorrows to me; he was both my kinsman and my lord."

He went forth bent on deeds of war, and stabbed one of the seafarers, dashing him to the ground dead. He urged his friends and comrades to advance.

Offa spoke, shaking his spear: "Alfwin, you have reminded us all of our duty. Now our lord lies on the ground, and each of us must encourage the other to fight as long as he can bear weapons, sword and spear. Godric, cowardly son of Odda, has betrayed us all. When they saw him ride forth on the spirited war horse, a great many men thought that it was our lord, and the people on the battlefield were divided, the shield-wall broken. May his deeds come to a bad end, since he caused so many men to flee."

Leofson spoke, raising his protecting shield, and answered: "I swear that I shall not flee from here so much as one footstep, but will go forward to avenge my lord and friend in battle. Never shall the men of Stourmere reproach me, saying that when my patron had fallen I came home lordless, fleeing the battle: rather shall I perish by the point of an iron weapon." Angrily he advanced, scorning flight.

Then Dunnere spoke; shaking his spear, the simple peasant called out to them all, urging every man to avenge Byrhtnoth:

"He who wishes to avenge his lord on the enemy host may not turn aside nor worry about saving his own life!"

They went forward, heedless of their lives. The band of household retainers, fierce spearmen, fought grimly, praying to God that they might avenge their lord and friend and bring about the death of their enemies. A hostage came to their aid eagerly; his name was Ashferth, Ecglaf's son, and he came of a hard-fighting Northumbrian family. He did not flinch from the war-play, but shot forth arrows continually: now he shot into a shield, now he pierced a man, and now and again he dealt a wound, as long as he could bear weapons.

Edward the tall still stood at the forefront of the battle line, ready and eager, vowing that he would not flee so much as a foot; never would he turn to the rear, where his leader lay. He broke the enemy shield-wall and fought until he had worthily avenged his lord on the seamen, before he lay among the slaughtered. Like him, the noble retainer Ethelric, Sigebyrht's brother, fought keenly; and many others cleft the shields fiercely and defended themselves boldly.

A shield burst, and shattered mail sang a terrible song: Offa struck down his viking attacker; he fell to the ground, but Gadd's kinsman also fell—Offa was cut down in battle. But he had fulfilled the vows he had made to his lord, when he had promised that either they would both ride home safely to the manor or both fall on the battlefield, wounded to death. He lay near his lord, as befitted a noble retainer.

Shields clashed and the vikings advanced, enraged, in the battle; many a spear went through a doomed body. Wistan, Thurstan's son, went forward, fighting against the enemy. Wighelm's kinsman killed three in the midst of the throng before he lay down among the dead. The battle raged; some stood firm, others fell, weary with wounds—the dead fell on the earth. Oswold and Edwold continually encouraged the men; both the brothers bade their kinsmen to hold fast there in the time of need, and to make use of their weapons without weakening.

Now Byrhtwold, an old retainer, spoke, raising his shield; shaking his spear, he boldly told the men: "Courage shall be the firmer, heart the keener, spirit the greater, as our might lessens.

Here lies our leader, quite destroyed; the good man lies in the dust. He who now thinks to leave the battle shall always mourn. I am advanced in years; I shall not go, for I intend to lie by the side of my dear lord."

So also did Godric, Ethelgar's son, call all of them to battle. Again and again he bore down on the vikings with his deadly spear as he rode foremost among the people, hewing and laying low the enemy, until he fell in battle. That was not the Godric who fled from the battle . . . .

--⊰ THE WANDERER ⊱--

"Often the lonely man abides the grace of God, the mercy of the Creator, though his hands have had to stir the frosty sea, and for a long time he may have had to tread the paths of exile over watery ways. Fate is inexorable," said the Wanderer, thinking of hardships he had endured, of deadly combats and the fall of beloved kin.

"Often I have had to mourn my sorrows alone in the early morning. There is no one now alive to whom I could tell my inmost thoughts. I know, indeed, that it is a good custom for an earl to bridle his feelings firmly and control his heart, whatever he may think. A disheartened man cannot withstand fate, nor can a troubled mind be of help. Therefore those who wish to be praiseworthy often suppress sad thoughts, keeping them deep in their breast. Thus I should fetter my inmost thoughts, which are often miserably sad: I am far from my native land and cut off from noble kindred, since the time, long ago, when I covered my lord with dark earth and mournfully departed over the sea. Chilled with sadness for lack of a hall, I went in search of a new lord, looking for a mead-hall near or far where I might find someone who knew of my people, or might comfort me, a friendless man, and receive me pleasantly.

"He who has no friendly protector knows what a cruel companion sorrow is. The paths of exile await him, not wrought gold; bitter pangs, and not earthly riches. He remembers comrades in the hall and the treasure he received, and how his generous lord accustomed him to feasting in his youth. But all joy

95

came to an end. So he who must long be deprived of his beloved lord's counsels knows how, when he is in the bonds of both sorrow and sleep, in his wretched solitude he thinks he embraces his lord, laying his hand and head on his knee in homage, as he used to do in former days when he enjoyed his lord's bounty; but then he awakens and finds himself alone and friendless, seeing nothing but dark waves and the sea birds bathing, spreading their feathers, in frost and snow falling mingled with hail. Then the wounds of the heart are heavier to bear, sore with longing for his dear lord. His sorrow is redoubled when the memory of kinsmen passes before his mind—he greets them joyously, eagerly beholding his comrades, but they swim off again. The spirits floating there do not bring him familiar voices. His care is renewed as he must frequently direct his weary mind over the sea.[1]

"Indeed, there does not seem to be any reason in the world why my mind should not become gloomy when I consider the lives of earls, and how bold young retainers no longer stand on the floor of the hall. Every day this Middle-Earth falters and fails. A man cannot become wise until he has spent many years in the realms of this world. The wise man must be patient, and not too hot tempered or too hasty of speech, neither too weak in battle nor too heedless, too fearful nor too merry, too greedy for wealth, nor too quick to boast, before he is quite certain. A man should wait and not make a vow until he is sure that his resolve is firm.

"The thinking man will know how desolate it must be when all this world's wealth stands waste, as now in many places all over the world there stand walls beaten by the wind and covered with frost, storm-battered remains that once were dwellings. The wine hall falls in ruins, and its ruler lies shorn of all joys; the band of proud retainers has all fallen by the wall. War took off some, sweeping them on; one was carried off over the high seas by

---

[1] Some readers feel that this poem, aside from remarks obviously those of the poet himself, is a monologue—as it is punctuated in this rendering. But others see it as a dialogue, or something near to it. It is possible that the first speaker (the Wanderer) ends his speech here, and the rest is the answer of the "wise man." Another reading considers the Wanderer's speech to include the next two sentences, and assigns the rest, except for the lament beginning "where is the horse," to the poet.

a bird of prey, and the gray wolf shared in the death of another; one was buried in a grave by a sad-faced earl. The Creator of men so laid waste to this region that the work of giants of old stands empty and silent.

"The wise man who carefully considers these ruined walls and this dark life remembers from the past a multitude of battles, and says, 'Where is the horse now, and where is the young rider? Where is the ruler, the giver of treasure? Where are the seats at the banquet? Where are the joys of the hall? Alas, for the bright cup and the mailed warrior; alas, for the glory of the lord! Their time has departed, vanished under shades of night, as if it had never been. Now no trace remains of the band of comrades but a wall, wondrously high, decorated with serpentine markings. Strong spears, weapons greedy for slaughter, destroyed the earls. They met their fate. Now storms beat against the stony slopes, snow covers the ground with wintry tumult, when the shadow of night darkens, and spitefully sends forth rough showers of hail from the north; all is bleak in the realms of earth. The workings of fate change the world under the heavens. Here wealth is transitory; here friends are transitory; here a man is transitory; here a woman is transitory, and all this earthly dwelling becomes empty.' "

So the wise man pondered in his heart, as he sat apart by himself in meditation. Praiseworthy is he who keeps his good faith. A man should never make his feelings known too quickly, before he knows how to find a remedy and can bring it about with fortitude. All will be well for the earl who seeks his grace and comfort from the Father in Heaven, where there is security for us all.

--⸗⸹{ DEOR }⸹⸗--

Weland,[1] sorely hindered, knew wretchedness; the staunch hero
endured trouble, with sorrow and longing for his only compan-
ions. Misery was his lot, persecution as bitter as winter, when
Nithhad fettered him, laying the better man in bonds of supple
sinew. That passed by; this may, too.

The death of her brothers was not so heavy a burden in the
breast of Beadohild as her own trouble, for she saw clearly that
she grew great with child. She dreaded what was to come of this.
That passed by; this may, too.

We have heard that the lamentations of Mathhild,[2] Geat's
lady, became so boundless that her sorrowful love robbed her of
all sleep. That passed by; this may, too.

Theodoric,[3] as many knew, occupied the city of the Merings for
thirty years. That passed by; this may, too.

[1] The legendary Germanic smith. King Nithhad, coveting his work, tried to
keep him a prisoner by hamstringing him (thus fettering him "in bonds of
supple sinew"). He took revenge by killing Nithhad's sons (and presenting
the king with artifacts made of their skulls and teeth) and seducing his
daughter, Beadohild, then escaped with the aid of wings (like Daedalus),
leaving Beadohild pregnant. However, after Nithhad died of chagrin, Weland
married Beadohild.

[2] Apparently a reference to the story of a bride who foresaw that she
would drown on her wedding journey. However, in one version at least,
when she did indeed fall into the destined river, her husband (Geat) was
able to rescue her miraculously.

[3] Possibly the Ostrogoth (fl. 500), known in German legend as Dietrich von
Bern; or the reference may be to a less well-known Frankish king of the same
period. In either case, the meaning is obscure: either the Merings—whoever
they may have been—suffered because Theodoric conquered them, or, con-
versely, Theodoric suffered because he was in exile among the Merings.

We have been told of the wolfish mind of Ermanaric,[4] who ruled far and wide over the Goths: he was a grim king. Many of the people sat bowed by sorrow, expecting still more troubles, and often wished his kingdom overthrown. That passed by; this may, too.

When a man sits grief stricken, deprived of all joy and gloomy at heart, it seems to him that his troubles are never ending. Then he may reflect that throughout this world the wise Lord[5] continually turns about, now showing grace and certain joy to many a man, now to some a measure of misery. This I can say about myself: for a while I was the Hedening's minstrel, and dear to their lord; Deor was my name. For many winters I served my gracious master, until Heorrenda, the skillful singer, was granted the land which the prince had formerly given to me. That passed by;[6] this may, too.

[4] Historical king of the Ostrogoths (d. ca. 375); in Germanic narrative, he often (but not always) appears as a bloodthirsty tyrant.

[5] Capitalization of "lord" is, of course, editorial; the phrase is open to interpretation. For example, the "lord" referred to could also be a terrestrial ruler, such as the one Deor served (referred to a few lines further on), who also turned his favor first to one man, then to another.

[6] In the earlier stanzas, this refrain refers to the passing of hard times in stories which ended happily: "that" refers to the hardships endured by Weland, Beadohild, etc., and "this" to the speaker's own hardships, i.e., the loss of the favor of the (legendary) lord of the Hedenings. The last line also suggests that the speaker's difficulties will pass, but apparently with a change of reference: here, "that" seems to refer to the *good* times which have passed; hence, he concludes, since God continually changes the world, his bad times ("this") will also come to an end.

THE DREAM OF THE ROOD

Listen, and I will tell you the most marvelous of dreams, which came to me in the middle of the night when the voices of men were stilled in sleep. It seemed to me that I saw an extraordinary tree, brightest of all beams, towering in the air, bathed in light. That beacon was covered with gold and lovely gems; some stood at its base, on the surface of the earth, and five more gleamed on the crossbeam. Hosts of angels, eternally fair, kept watch over it. This was no gallows for a common criminal: holy spirits gazed upon it—men, all over the earth, and all this glorious creation.

Strange and rare was the great tree, and I, a sinner, stained by my faults, saw the heavenly tree, splendidly arrayed, shining, beautiful, adorned with gold and covered with a splendor of gems. Yet through that gold I could perceive the earlier ordeal of the wretched, for it began to bleed on the right side. I was stricken with grief, terrified at that fair vision. I saw that brilliant beacon change array and color, for now it was moist and wet, drenched with a flow of blood, now it was adorned with treasure.

But as I lay there I gazed, troubled, for a long time at the Savior's tree, until I heard it call out, and the best of all wood spoke these words:

"It was long ago—well I remember!—when I was cut down at the edge of the forest and taken away from my trunk. Strong enemies took me there and made a spectacle of me, ordering me to lift up their criminals. Then men bore me on their shoulders until they set me on a hill; enemies enough made me fast there.

"Then I saw the Lord of mankind, hastening eagerly, for He wished to mount up upon me. I did not dare to bend or break against the Lord's command, when I saw the surface of the earth tremble. Though I could have dashed down all the enemies, I stood firm.

"The young Hero—who was God almighty—stripped Himself. Strong and resolute, He ascended onto the high gallows while many beheld His courage, when He wished to free mankind. I trembled when the Warrior embraced me, but I did not dare bow down to the earth or fall to the surface of the ground; I had to stand steadfast. I was raised as the Rood; I bore up the powerful King, Lord of Heaven, and I did not dare to bend.

"They drove dark nails through me: the open wounds, inflicted in malice, are still visible. Yet I dared not injure any of those who mocked us both. I was wet with blood, drenched with the flow from the Man's side when He had yielded up His spirit. Many cruel blows of fate I endured on that hill! I saw the God of hosts grievously stretched out. Darkness covered the bright radiance of the Ruler's body. Shadows lowered, dark under the clouds. All creation wept and lamented the King's death. Christ was crucified.

"But now from the distance men came hurrying to the Prince. I witnessed all that. I was sore troubled with grief, but I bowed down to the men's hands, humbly and eagerly. Then they took almighty God and lifted Him up from the heavy punishment. The warriors left me standing covered with blood, badly wounded by sharp-pointed weapons. They laid down the weary-limbed Warrior and stood by the head of His body, beholding there Heaven's Lord. There He rested a while, spent after the great ordeal. Still within view of His bane,[1] they began to build Him a sepulchre. They carved it of bright stone, and set the Ruler of victories in it; the mourners began to sing a dirge as evening approached, until time came for them to go off, wearily, leaving the glorious Lord to rest there with scant company.

---

[1] Probably refers to the Cross, as unwilling instrument of Christ's death.

"But still we[2] stood there in that same place, mourning, for a long time. The voices of the warriors faded away. The body, fair dwelling of the soul, grew cold. Then someone came to fell us all to the earth—a terrible fate; they buried us in a deep pit. But the Lord's friends and servants[3] found me there, and adorned me with gold and silver.

"Now, friends, you must understand that I have endured the work of evildoers and suffered terrible sorrows. And now the time has come when men on earth honor me far and wide, and all this glorious creation prays to this sign. On me God's Son suffered a while; therefore I now rise up glorious under Heaven, and can heal those who hold me in awe. Once I was made the worst of punishments before I opened the right way of life to men of all tongues. Behold, then the Father of glories, Guardian of the heavenly Kingdom, honored me above all the wood of the forest, just as the almighty God also honored His mother, Mary, over all womankind, for all men's sake.

"Now, dear man, I bid you tell this vision to men, revealing to them that this is the Tree of Glory on which almighty God suffered for mankind's many sins and Adam's deeds of old, when He tasted death; nevertheless, the Lord arose in His great might to succor men. Then He ascended into Heaven. He shall return again to earth, seeking out mankind, on Doomsday: the Lord Himself, almighty God, shall come with His angels, and then He who is Judge over all shall judge, giving to each according to what he has earned here in this transitory life. None can then be unafraid of the Ruler's words, for He shall ask of the multitude where that man is who in the name of the Lord would partake of bitter death as He did before on the Cross. And they shall be afraid, and unable to imagine what they can answer to Christ.

"But neither need any man be unduly afraid who has borne in his heart the best of tokens, for through the rood every soul who desires to dwell with the Ruler shall come to the Kingdom from his earthly path."

---

[2] The three crosses (though the other two are not mentioned before, they are clearly included in the following lines).
[3] A reference to St. Helena and the Invention (finding) of the True Cross.

Then I eagerly prayed to the rood, in joyful mood, alone as I was. My heart urged me forth on the way,[4] and I felt a great longing. My greatest joy is the hope that I may often seek out the Tree of victory and duly honor it. I have few powerful friends here on earth, for they have departed and left the joys of this world behind, seeking the King of Glory, and dwell now in Heaven with God the Father, in glory; each day I look for the time when the Lord's rood, which I beheld here on earth before, will fetch me from this transitory life, and bring me to where there is great gladness, heavenly joy; where the Lord's people sit at the feast and there is everlasting bliss; where I may then dwell in glory, and fully share in the rejoicing of the saints.

May the Lord be my friend, He who once suffered on the gallows-tree here on earth for man's sin. He redeemed us, and granted us life in a heavenly home. Joy was restored to those who had endured the fires of Hell. The Son, mighty in battle, came back victorious, when the mighty Ruler returned in victory with a great multitude of spirits into God's kingdom, and the angels and all the saints who dwelt in glory in Heaven rejoiced that their Leader, almighty God, came into His native realm.

[4] I.e., "the right way of life," the way to heaven, which the Cross has just explained that it "opened."

⸻⟨ JUDITH ⟩⸻

Judith enjoyed the grace of the glorious Lord. The supreme Judge protected her in her greatest need: Ruler of all creatures, He defended her when she was in the highest peril. Because she had always had firm faith in the Almighty, the Father in Heaven granted her a glorious favor.

It is said that Holofernes sent out invitations to a sumptuous banquet, bidding all his chief thanes to come drink with him. The warriors hurried to obey their leader, and came to their powerful lord. Then, on the fourth day, deep-minded Judith, a lady lovely as an elf, came to him.

The bold warriors—comrades in trouble—sat at the feast in their pride, drinking wine. Deep bowls were carried along the benches again and again, and those that sat in the hall were well provided with full cups and flagons. Many fierce fighting men who drank there were doomed to death, though the great and terrible lord did not know this. Holofernes rejoiced as the wine was poured: he laughed and he roared, and the clamor resounded so that men far away could hear him storming and yelling, as, flushed with mead, he urged all his guests to shout lustily.

All day long the proud chieftain drenched his retainers with wine, until they fell in a swoon—so drunk that they lay as if dead, drained of all their senses. Thus the commander ordered the guests to be served, until the shadows of night approached; then the evil man called for the noble lady, in her rich attire, to be fetched to his bed. Quickly his retainers obeyed their chief and noisily made their way to the guest hall, where they found keen-witted Judith. And quickly the warriors led the splendid maiden to the high pavilion where powerful Holofernes, hateful to the Savior, always rested at night.

A beautiful curtain hung around the prince's bed, so that that baleful warrior could look through and see anyone who came in, but no man could see him unless he should wish to consult one, and order him to come nearer. Quickly the men brought Judith to this bed, then went to announce to their lord that the hallowed woman was in his pavilion. The bold leader rejoiced, for he intended to defile the bright lady with foul sin. But the heavenly Judge would not allow that: the Lord of hosts restrained him.

The wicked lecher left to go to his bed, where he was to lose his might before the night was past. He was about to receive the reward he had earned through all his deeds when he dwelled in this world under the skies: that is, a bitter ending of his life on earth. Now he was so drunk with wine that he fell on his bed senseless. The warriors, who had drunk their fill, quickly left the bedchamber. For the last time they had led the hateful tyrant to bed.

Now the Savior's handmaiden, glorious Judith, considered in her mind how she might best take the terrible man's life before the foul sinner woke up. The curly-haired maiden took a sharp sword, hardened in battle, and drew it from the sheath with her right hand, calling on the Guardian of Heaven, savior of the world, saying: "God of creation, Son of the Almighty, Comforter —I beseech Thee for Thy grace, blessed Trinity! My heart is on fire and my mind is troubled, weighed down with care. O Ruler of Heaven, grant me victory and firm faith, so that I can cut this tyrant down with my sword; grant me salvation, Ruler of men. Never have I had greater need of Thy mercy. Avenge, mighty Lord, my grief and hatred."

The Judge of all men inspired her with courage, as He will any earthly man who wisely seeks His help, with true belief. Her mind was filled with hope. She took the heathen firmly by the hair, drew him towards her with her hands, and skillfully placed the hateful man in a suitable position so that she could easily

deal with him. The curly-haired maid struck her hated enemy
with the gleaming sword and cut half-way through his neck, as he
lay there insensible, drunk and wounded. But he was not yet
quite dead; the brave lady struck sharply a second time, and the
heathen hound's head rolled off on the floor. The foul body lay
dead; his spirit fled into the dark abyss to endure shameful pun-
ishments for ever after: tortured in the coils of serpents, bound in
torments, painfully imprisoned in hellfire after death. Nor had
he any cause to hope for release from the shadows in which he
was trapped: never could he leave the den of serpents. He shall
abide there forever, world without end, in the darkness, deprived
of all hope and joy.

Judith had won glory in battle—God, Lord of Heaven, had
given her the victory. Swiftly the wise maiden picked up the
bloody head, and put it into the sack in which her attendant—a
fair and virtuous lady—had brought food for them both; Judith
gave it, with its gory burden, into the prudent girl's hand to bear
home. Then the two courageous women left the place, leaving
the camp of the invading army, and went on triumphantly until
they were near enough to see the glittering walls of the beautiful
city, Bethuliam. They followed the roadway until they came to
the city gate, where warriors kept watch over the city, as brave
Judith had instructed them to before when the wise maiden had
gone on her journey, leaving her anxious people behind. Now
the lady, so dear to her people, had returned.

She told one of the men from the great city to come to her
quickly and let her in through the gate in the wall, and she spoke
these words to the victorious people: "I bring you tidings for
which thanksgiving is due: you need no longer mourn. The Lord
is gracious to you. It has been made manifest to the world that
you are about to be given marvelous success and glory in place of
the afflictions you have long suffered."

The inhabitants of the city were glad when they heard her
message over the high wall; the army rejoiced, and the people
hurried to the gates of the fortress, men and women together in
great multitudes—companies, troops, thronged and ran towards
the Lord's maiden by the thousands, young and old. The spirits
of all the men in the city were lightened when they learned that

Judith had returned to her home, and with great reverence they quickly let her in.

The noble lady told her handmaid to bring out the warrior's head and display it to the people of the city as a bloody token of her success in battle; she spoke to them, saying: "Brave men, here for all to gaze on is the head of the most hateful heathen, dead Holofernes! He did us grievous harm, and planned to inflict still greater blows: but God did not grant him longer life in which to harrass us. With God's help, I took his life. Now I ask every warrior in the town to go to battle. As soon as the glorious King of creation sends bright light from the east, bring forth your shields and bear them forward before your mail and bright helms into the enemy camp—fell their leaders with your shining swords! Your enemies are doomed to death, and you shall win fame and glory in battle, as the mighty Lord has shown you through my hand."

Soon a bold band of men were prepared for battle, and, bearing triumphal banners, went forth from the holy city, helmets gleaming in the light of that same dawn. Shields rang, resounding loudly. The lank wolf in the wood heard and rejoiced, and the dark raven, greedy for carrion: they knew that the warriors would give them their fill of the doomed. Behind them flew the dusky dewy-winged eagle, eager for prey; the horny-beaked birds sang a battle song.

Protected by their hollow shields, the warriors who before endured the insolence of the foreigners now advanced to battle. The heathens were well repaid for that abuse when the Hebrews had come under their battle standards into the Assyrian camp, letting fly showers of arrows, strong and stinging, from their bows. Storming loudly they sent their spears against the foe; they advanced, stern and resolute, against the hated invaders of their native land, and urgently aroused their ancient enemies, who lay weary after the mead drinking. Pulling their good swords from their sheaves, they struck at the evil Assyrians and spared no one of the enemy army, high or low—none of the men they caught were left alive.

Thus through the morning they pursued the enemy, until it became quite clear to the captains of the enemy army that the

Hebrews were dealing violent strokes with their swords. They went to tell the chief leaders, arousing the warriors to announce the fearful tidings to them; they brought word of the morning's terror to them where they lay wearied with mead.

The doomed men shook off sleep and thronged in alarm to the pavilion of baleful Holofernes, intending to tell him at once about the battle before the might of the Hebrews was upon him. But they all thought that their chief, the lecherous tyrant, lay with the bright maiden, noble Judith, in the lovely tent, and none dared awaken the terrible warrior or inquire how he had fared with the holy maiden. The force drew nearer; the Hebrew people fought on, fiercely repaying old grudges with bright swords. The glory of Assyria was destroyed in that day's work, and all its pride abased.

Disconsolately, the men stood around their lord's pavilion. They all started to give coughs; then they cried out aloud and gnashed their teeth, seeing the end of all their prosperity, suffering to their very teeth: their glory was at an end—all their success and deeds of valor were to come to nothing. Thus they tried to awaken their lord, but with no success. Then at long last one of the warriors became bold enough to venture into the pavilion itself—of necessity—and there he found on the bed his lord, lying pale and lifeless. At that sight he fell to the floor, tearing his hair, and raged and lamented, crying to the warriors who stood outside, "Our destruction is upon us; here we can see that the time has come when we shall be totally lost and must perish together in battle. Here, cut down by the sword, beheaded, lies our leader."

In desolation they cast their weapons down and scattered in flight. But the mighty fighters pursued and waylaid them, until the greater part of the army lay dead on the field of victory, cut down by the sword, and left for the enjoyment of the wolves and the pleasure of birds greedy for carrion. Those of the hateful army that still lived fled, with the Hebrew army on their tracks, glorious in victory: the Lord God almighty had given them bountiful help. With their bright swords the valiant warriors cut a path through the troop of hated foes, hewing shields and cleaving the shield-wall. The Hebrew men fought in a frenzy of rage, thanes who were eager to use their spears, and the greater part of the hated Assyrians fell there in the dust. Few returned alive to their native land.

Finally the brave men turned back, retracing their way among the reeking corpses. The countrymen had plenty of opportunity to take bloodstained spoils from the hated enemies; they gathered beautiful ornaments from their dead foes, shields and broadswords, shining helmets, and all kinds of valuable treasures. The defenders of the homeland had gloriously defeated their enemies on the battlefield, for their swords had laid the old foes to rest. Those who had been in life the most hateful to them of all living races lay where they had fallen. For a full month the triumphant nation, most renowned of peoples, carried off helmets and daggers, shining mail, warlike trappings decorated with gold, and more splendid treasures than any tongue can tell into the bright city of Bethuliam. All of this had been won by the courage of the warriors who had gone into battle, going forth boldly under their banners, through the counsel of the prudent maid Judith.

As her own reward, the warriors brought Judith the sword of Holofernes, his bloody helmet and his ample mail, adorned with red gold, and every bit of the treasure that was the private property of the proud leader—all that they gave to the bright lady. For all this Judith praised the glory of God, who had given her honor and glory on earth as well as a heavenly reward, victory in heaven itself, because she had true faith in the Almighty. She never doubted that in the end she would gain the reward she had long yearned for. For this, thanks be to God, honor and glory forever to Him who in His mercy created the wind and the air, the heavens and the spacious earth, the raging waters and the joys of heaven.

⊸≼ THE SEAFARER ≽⊷

TRANSLATED BY EZRA POUND[1]

May I for my own self song's truth reckon,
Journey's jargon, how I in harsh days
Hardship endured oft.
Bitter breast-cares have I abided,
Known on my keel many a care's hold,
And dire sea-urge, and there I oft spent
Narrow nightwatch nigh the ship's head
While she tossed close to cliffs. Coldly afflicted,
My feet were by frost benumbed.
Chill its chains are; chafing sighs
Hew my heart round and hunger begot
Mere-weary mood. Lest man know not
That he on dry land loveliest liveth,
List how I, care-wretched, on ice-cold sea,
Weathered the winter, wretched outcast
Deprived of my kinsmen;
Hung with hard ice-flakes, where hail-scur flew,
There I heard naught save the harsh sea
And ice-cold wave, at whiles the swan cries,
Did for my games the gannet's clamour,
Sea-fowls' loudness was for me laughter
The mews' singing all my mead-drink.
Storms, on the stone-cliffs beaten, fell on the stern
In icy feathers; full oft the eagle screamed
With spray on his pinion
                        Not any protector
May make merry man faring needy.
This he little believes, who aye in winsome life

[1] From Ezra Pound, *Personae*. Copyright 1926, 1953 by Ezra Pound. Reprinted by permission of New Directions Publishing Corporation.

Abides 'mid burghers some heavy business,
Wealthy and wine-flushed, how I weary oft
Must abide above brine
Neareth nightshade, snoweth from north,
Frost froze the land, hail fell on earth then,
Corn of the coldest. Nathless there knocketh now
The heart's thought that I on high streams
The salt-wavy tumult traverse alone.
Moaneth alway my mind's lust
That I fare forth, that I afar hence
Seek out a foreign fastness
For this there's no mood-lofty man over earth's midst,
Not though he be given his good, but will have in his youth greed;
Nor his deed to the daring, nor his king to the faithful
But shall have his sorrow for sea-fare
Whatever his lord will.
He hath not heart for harping, nor in ring-having
Nor winsomeness to wife, nor world's delight
Nor any whit else save the wave's slash,
Yet longing comes upon him to fare forth on the water.
Bosque taketh blossom, cometh beauty of berries,
Fields to fairness, land fares brisker,
All this admonisheth man eager of mood,
The heart turns to travel so that he then thinks
On flood-ways to be far departing.
Cuckoo calleth with gloomy crying,
He singeth summerward, bodeth sorrow,
The bitter heart's blood. Burgher knows not—
He the prosperous man—what some perform
Where wandering them widest draweth.
So that but now my heart burst from my breastlock,
My mood 'mid the mere-flood,
Over the whale's acre, would wander wide.
On earth's shelter cometh oft to me,
Eager and ready, the crying lone-flyer,
Whets for the whale-path the heart irresistibly,
O'er tracks of ocean; seeing that anyhow
My lord deems to me this dead life
On loan and on land, I believe not

That any earth-weal eternal standeth
Save there be somewhat calamitous
That, ere a man's tide go, turn it to twain.
Disease or oldness or sword-hate
Beats out the breath from doom-gripped body.
And for this, every earl whatever, for those speaking after—
Laud of the living, boasteth some last word,
That he will work ere he pass onward,
Frame on the fair earth 'gainst foes his malice,
Daring ado,...
So that all men shall honour him after
And his laud beyond them remain 'mid the English,
Aye, for ever, a lasting life's blast,
Delight 'mid the doughty.

                                  Days little durable,
And all the arrogance of earthen riches,
There come now no kings nor Caesars
Nor gold-giving lords like those gone.
Howe'er in earth most magnified,
Whoe'er lived in life most lordliest,
Drear all this excellence, delights undurable!
Waneth the watch, but the world holdeth.
Tomb hideth trouble. The blade is layed low.
Earthly glory ageth and seareth.
No man at all going the earth's gait,
But age fares against him, his face paleth,
Grey-haired he groaneth, knows gone companions,
Lordly men, are to earth o'ergiven,
Nor may he then the flesh-cover, whose life ceaseth,
Nor eat the sweet nor feel the sorry,
Nor stir hand nor think in mid heart,
And though he strew the grave with gold,
His born brothers, their buried bodies
Be an unlikely treasure hoard.[2]

[2] Pound omits the specifically Christian conclusion of the poem (thought by some scholars to be an epilogue—like *The Wanderer*, *The Seafarer* can be interpreted as representing more than one speaker), just as within the body of the poem, he has changed or eliminated references to God, the afterlife, etc.

·{ APPENDIX A }·

The spelling of the passage on the following page has been partially "normalized" for consistency. E.g., the two sounds spelled *th* in Modern English are differentiated: þ is used for the sound heard in *thin* and *bath*, and ð for the sound in *then* and *bathe*. For manuscript spelling, see Klaeber's text, or that of Dobbie or Wrenn, as listed in the Bibliography, p. 118.

On the page facing the passage is a phonetic transcription, intended to be rendered according to standard American English pronunciation for the given spellings, for the convenience of those who are unfamiliar with the International Phonetic Alphabet. The careful reader should come close enough if he tries to stress only the syllables marked [/], indicating primary stress, and [\], indicating secondary (but almost as strong) stress. Syllable divisions for words of more than one syllable are indicated with hyphens, but note that some syllables (such as *beya*) are practically disyllabic. Dots indicate a slight pause. To achieve a rhythmic reading, give each of the four syllable-groups (indicated by spacing) of a line approximately equal time (cf. Introduction, p. 5).

A literal prose translation of the passage appears on page 116.

Him þā Scyld ȝewāt   to ȝescæphwīle
felahrōr feran   on Frēan wǣre;
hī hine þā ætbǣron   tō brimes faroðe,
swǣse ȝesīðas,   swā hē selfa bæd,
þenden wordum wēold   wine Scyldinga—
lēof landfruma   lange āhte.
þǣr æt hȳðe stōd   hringedstefna
īsiȝ ond ūtfūs,   æðelinges fær;
ālēdon þā   lēofne þēoden,
bēaga bryttan   on bearm scipes,
mǣrne be mǣste.   þǣr wæs māðma fela
of feorweȝum   frætwa ȝelǣded;
ne hȳrde ic cȳmlīcor   cēol ȝeȝyrwan
hildewǣpnum   ond heaðowǣdum,
billum ond byrnum;   him on bearme læȝ
māðma mænigo,   þā him mid scoldon
on flōdes ǣht   feor ȝewītan.
Nalæs hī hine lǣssan   lācum tēodan,
þēodȝestrēonum,   þon þā dydon,
þē hine æt frumsceafte   forþ onsendon
ǣnne ofer ȳðe   umborwesende.
þā ȝȳt hīe him āsetton   seȝen gyldenne
hēah ofer hēafod,   lēton holm beran,
ȝēafon on gārsecg;   him wæs ȝēomor sefa,
murnende mōd.   Men ne cunnon
secgan tō sōðe,   selerǣdende,
hæleþ under heofenum,   hwā þām hlæste onfēng.

. . Him thah Shield yuh-wot . . toe yuh- shap-wheel-uh
fel-a-hrore fare-on on Frayan wear-uh
he hin-uh thah at- bare-on toe brim-is far-othe-uh
swy-za yuh- seethe-es . . swah hay sel-va bad
. . then-din wor-dum wayld win-uh Shield-ing-ga.
layf . lond-frum-a long-guh okt-uh.
. . There at heethe-uh stode hring-ged stev-na
eez-y ond oot-foos ath-el-ing-gus far . .
ah-lay-don thah . . layv-nuh thayo-den .
beya-ga brit-ton . . on bearm ship-is .
mare-nuh bey mast-uh . . There was mahthe-ma fel-a
. . . of fare-way-um frat-wa yuh- lad-ed.
nuh heer-duh ich keem-leek-or tchayol yuh- yeer-wan
hil-duh- wap-num ond hathe-o way-dum .
bil-lum ond beer-num . . him on bearm-uh lay
mahthe-ma men-i-go . . thah him mid shol-don
. . . on flode-is akt fare yuh- weet-on.
Nah-les he hin-uh lase-son lah-kum tayo-don
thayo-dya- strayo-num . . . thon thah did-on
they hin-uh at frum-shaft-uh forth on- send-on
ann-nuh over euthe-uh . umb'r- wez-end-uh.
Thah yeet he-uh him ah- set-ton sey-yen gil-den-nuh
hayac over hayd-vod . . lay-ton holm ber-on.
yayve-on on gar-sedge . . him was yo-mor se-va .
moor-nin-duh mode . . Men nuh kun-non
sedge-on toe sothe-uh . sel-a- rad-en-duh
hal-eth un-der heh-ven-um . . hwah tham hlast-uh on-feng.

Then Scyld departed at [the] fated time, [the] very strong [man], [to] go into [the] keeping [of the] Lord; they then bore him to [the] sea's current, dear companions, as he himself bade, when [the] friendly lord [of the] Scyldings wielded words—[the] dear land's prince ruled long. There at harbor waited [a] ring-prowed [ship], icy and eager to set out, [a] prince's vessel; [they] laid down there [their] dear lord, [the] giver [of] rings, in [the] bosom [of the] ship, [the] glorious [one] by the mast. There was brought many treasures, ornaments, from far ways; nor have I heard [of a] ship more beautifully equipped [with] battle-weapons and war-garments, swords and byrnies; on his bosom lay many treasures, which should go far with him in [the] power [of the] flood. Not at all did they give him lesser gifts, nation's treasures, than did those who in [the] beginning sent him forth alone over [the] waves as a child. Then besides they placed [a] golden banner high over [his] head, let [the] sea take [him], gave [him] into [the] ocean; their spirit was sad, mood mournful. Men could not say certainly, hall-counselors, warriors under [the] heavens, who received that load.

-◄{ APPENDIX B }►-

Genealogical Tables

THE DANES

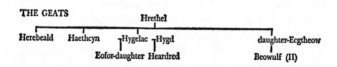

```
                        Scyld Scefing
                         Beowulf (I)
                          Healfdene
Heorogar              Hrothgar-Wealhtheow      Halga        daughter-Onela
Heoroweard                                    Hrothulf
            Hrethric Hrothmund Freawaru-Ingeld
```

THE GEATS

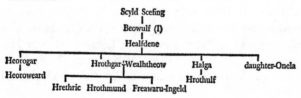

```
                          Hrethel
Herebeald    Haethcyn    Hygelac-Hygd              daughter-Ecgtheow
            Eofor-daughter Heardred               Beowulf (II)
```

THE SWEDES

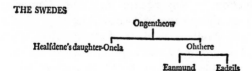

```
                    Ongentheow
        Healfdene's daughter-Onela      Ohthere
                                   Eanmund   Eadgils
```

117

-❧ BIBLIOGRAPHY ❧-

The first place to look for further information about *Beowulf* is the edition of the poem in Old English edited by Friedrich Klaeber (3rd ed.; New York: D. C. Heath & Co., 1950). The introduction, notes, bibliographies, and other apparatus will assist any serious inquirer, whether or not he reads Old English. Other useful recent editions are those edited by E. V. K. Dobbie (Vol. IV of *The Anglo-Saxon Poetic Records;* New York: Columbia University Press, 1953); C. L. Wrenn (rev. ed.; London: George Harrap & Co., 1958); and, in a normalized orthography, F. P. Magoun, Jr. (Cambridge, Mass.: Department of English of Harvard University, 1959).

Judith will be found in the editions of *Beowulf* edited by Dobbie and Magoun; several other Old English poems (including *Deor*) are included in Klaeber's edition. A well-annotated text containing all the short poems in the present volume except *Judith* is John C. Pope's *Seven Old English Poems* (Indianapolis: Bobbs-Merrill, 1966).

For background on the Anglo-Saxon period, Peter Hunter Blair, *An Introduction to Anglo-Saxon England* (Cambridge: The University Press, 1962; paperback available) is particularly recommended. Other standard works include R. H. Hodgkin, *History of the Anglo-Saxons* (3rd ed.; London: Oxford University Press, 1952; with valuable appendix by R. Bruce-Mitford); Sir Frank Stenton, *Anglo-Saxon England* (2nd ed.; Oxford: Clarendon Press, 1947); and Dorothy Whitelock, *The Beginnings of English Society* (London: Penguin, 1952).

Stanley B. Greenfield, *A Critical History of Old English Literature* (New York: New York University Press, 1965; Gotham Library paperback) is a good survey of the literature. A valuable collection of essays is *An Anthology of Beowulf Criticism,* ed. Lewis E. Nicholson (University of Notre Dame Press, 1963; paperback). Other important works on Beowulf include: Adrien Bonjour, *The Digressions in Beowulf* (Oxford: Blackwell, 1950); A. G. Brodeur, *The Art of Beowulf* (Berkeley: University of California Press, 1959); R. W. Chambers, *Beowulf, an Introduction to the Study of the Poem* (with supplement by C. L. Wrenn; 3rd ed.; Cambridge: The University Press, 1959); Ritchie Girvan, *Beowulf and the Seventh Century* (London: Methuen, 1935); W. W. Lawrence, *Beowulf and the Epic Tradition* (Cambridge, Mass.; Harvard University Press, 1928); John C. Pope, *The Rhythm of Beowulf* (rev. ed.; New Haven: Yale University Press, 1966; paperback); J. R. R. Tolkien, *Beowulf: the Monster and the Critics* (London: Oxford University Press, 1937; also in anthology ed. Nicholson, above); and Dorothy Whitelock, *The Audience of Beowulf* (Oxford: Clarendon Press, 1951).

For those interested in reading more medieval Germanic literature, much is available in translation. Among recent editions are *Eirik the Red and Other Icelandic Sagas,* trans. Gwyn Jones (London: Oxford University Press, 1961—the saga of King Hrolf, included in this volume, is particularly interesting to readers of *Beowulf* since it is a parallel version of some of the same stories); *Njal's Saga,* greatest of the Icelandic sagas, in two recent translations, those of Carl F. Bayerschmidt and Lee M. Hollander (New York: New York University Press, 1955) and Magnus Magnusson and Herman Pálson (Baltimore: Penguin, 1960); and *The Nibelungenlied,* trans. A. T. Hatto (Baltimore: Penguin, 1965; the "Introduction to a Second Reading" is highly recommended). The Everyman's Library series includes the *Nibelungenlied, The Laxdale Saga, The Saga of Grettir the Strong* (another analogue to *Beowulf*), and Snorri Sturluson's *Heimskringla.*